THE PARADOX OF ENOUGH

DOES SATISFACTION KILL PROGRESS?

TANMEEN MAKEN

ISBN
Paperback 979-8-89588-397-6
Hardcase 979-8-89673-420-8

Dedication

To my parents, Hardeep and Rani Maken, who taught me the meaning of hard work, humility, and unwavering love—your guidance has shaped every step of my journey.

To my wife, Deepti Maken, my anchor and my biggest cheerleader—your faith in me has been my greatest strength, and your love my constant inspiration.

To my children, Ruhveer and Raniah, who remind me every day of life's infinite possibilities—may you always chase your dreams with courage and curiosity.

This book is dedicated to the people who make my life meaningful and complete, and whose love inspires me to become the best version of myself every single day.

CONTENTS

In a world that never stops pushing us to achieve more, to do more, and to be more, where does one draw the line between fulfillment and ambition? Is true satisfaction the end of growth, or can contentment and progress coexist in harmony?

The Paradox of Enough – Does Satisfaction Kill Progress? is a deep dive into the complex interplay between contentment and the drive for more. Drawing on wisdom from ancient philosophies, modern psychology, and real-world stories, this book explores the timeless question: When is enough truly enough?

Through engaging chapters that dissect everything from the hedonic treadmill to the impact of social comparison and societal expectations, this book invites readers to reflect on their own relationship with growth and satisfaction. It challenges the belief that ambition must always come at the cost of inner peace and raises thought-provoking questions about the true cost of our unending quest for progress.

Whether you're striving for career success, searching for deeper personal fulfillment, or simply trying to find balance in a world obsessed with productivity, *The Paradox of Enough* offers a fresh perspective that will inspire you to rethink your priorities. With a narrative that seamlessly blends thought-provoking insights and practical wisdom, this book will leave you questioning the traditional definitions of success and inspire you to embrace a more balanced approach to life.

Prepare to embark on a journey that will make you pause, ponder, and ultimately redefine what it means to truly grow—without losing sight of what you already have.

SYNOPSIS

Title: ***The Paradox of Enough - Does Satisfaction Kill Progress?***

In a country like India, where tradition blends seamlessly with modern ambition, the quest for 'more' has become a defining trait. We see it every day—in bustling markets, in packed office spaces, in conversations over chai about new goals and aspirations. But amidst all this striving for progress, an age-old question lingers: *When is enough truly enough?*

This book doesn't pretend to have all the answers. Instead, it offers a space for readers to pause, reflect, and rethink the way they look at growth, success, and contentment. Through the lenses of philosophy, psychology, history, and culture, it delves into what drives our constant hunger for more and how we can balance it with the serenity of being satisfied with what we already have.

Chapter Highlights

1. **Definitions and Distinctions**

   This chapter lays the foundation, defining what contentment, satisfaction, progress, and growth mean—not just in theory, but in our everyday lives. How do we distinguish between wanting more out of ambition and craving more because we feel unfulfilled? How can we understand these concepts in a way that resonates with our own personal stories?

2. **Philosophical Perspectives**

   From the calming teachings of the Buddha to the stoic wisdom of Marcus Aurelius, and even modern existentialist musings, this chapter takes you on a journey through the thoughts of those who have pondered these ideas for centuries. It challenges readers to see satisfaction not as an endpoint but as a foundation for meaningful growth.

3. **Psychological Insights**
   Exploring the science of the mind, this chapter explores why we chase growth even when we've reached our goals. Concepts like Maslow's Hierarchy of Needs and the hedonic treadmill help us understand why 'enough' is such a tricky concept to grasp and why contentment sometimes seems like a mirage in the distance.

4. **Sociological Aspects**
   How do society and culture influence our ideas of success and satisfaction? This chapter explores how growing up in a world of constant comparisons shapes our view of ourselves and our achievements. It questions whether our drive for progress is truly our own or a reflection of what society expects from us.

5. **Economic Considerations**
   Can economic growth bring happiness, or does it just keep us chasing the next big thing? From Gross National Happiness to consumerism, this chapter analyses how our desire for more is often intertwined with the economic systems that fuel it.

6. **Biological and Evolutionary Perspectives**
   Is the pursuit of growth hardwired into us? This chapter looks at how our mind and biology influence our desires, explaining why we're always on the lookout for the next reward and how evolutionary forces have shaped our hunger for progress.

7. **Historical Examples**
   What can we learn from those who came before us? This chapter draws on historical case studies of individuals and societies that found their own balance—or failed to—and what those lessons mean for us today.

8. **Technological Impact**
   With technology reshaping our lives at lightning speed, this chapter examines how it influences our pursuit of satisfaction and growth. Does it make us happier, or does it keep us forever wanting more?

9. **Environmental Considerations**
   In a world facing environmental crises, how do we redefine growth? This chapter questions whether we can grow without consuming more than we should and how we can find contentment in a lifestyle that respects the planet.

10. **Personal Development**
    Offers practical advice on how to grow and improve ourselves without falling into the trap of never-ending ambition. Strategies include cultivating mindfulness, setting meaningful goals, and learning to appreciate where we are now, even as we strive for more.

11. **Creativity and Innovation**
    Discusses how feelings of discontent can drive creativity and innovation but warns against the burnout that can follow. It explores how we can channel our creative energy without losing ourselves in the process.

12. **Ethics and Morality**
    What are the moral implications of chasing growth at all costs? This chapter reflects on how to balance personal aspirations with social responsibility and ethical considerations.

13. **Future Projections**
    Looks ahead to what the future might hold. Will we continue chasing more, or will we redefine progress in a way that allows for true satisfaction? This chapter speculates on the changes in society's views on success and contentment in the years to come.

Conclusion: Finding Balance

The paradox of enough is something we all live with. Every time we achieve something we've worked hard for, there's a moment of satisfaction—followed by the inevitable question, "What's next?" This book isn't about finding the final answer to that question but about understanding why we ask it in the first place. It's about learning to embrace the journey, appreciate the present, and choose our paths with awareness and intention.

Who Should Read This Book?

This book is for anyone who has ever felt caught between being grateful for what they have and wanting to strive for more. It's for the go-getters, the dreamers, the overthinkers, and the ones who sometimes wonder if they're missing out on the peace that comes with contentment. Whether you're a professional chasing career goals, a student navigating expectations, or someone simply seeking clarity, *The Paradox of Enough - Does Satisfaction Kill Progress?* will offer you a fresh perspective on the pursuit of growth and fulfillment.

PREFACE

In India, a land of immense diversity and contrasts, the search for fulfillment takes on unique dimensions. From the tranquil villages where life moves at a gentle pace to the bustling cities where ambitions run high, Indians are caught in a dynamic interplay between ancient wisdom and modern aspirations. Here, the age-old teachings of contentment, as espoused in texts like the *Bhagavad Gita*, coexist with a relentless drive for growth and progress in a fast-changing global economy.

This book seeks to unravel the complex relationship between contentment and growth – two forces that often seem to be at odds with each other, yet are intricately connected. As a country, we find ourselves standing at the crossroads of these competing desires. Our cultural heritage tells us to seek inner peace and be content with what we have, while our economic development urges us to strive for more, reach greater heights, and achieve success at every turn.

The question is: Can we balance these two seemingly opposing forces? Can we pursue progress without sacrificing our sense of peace and satisfaction? Is contentment truly the end of growth, or is it a foundation from which true growth can begin?

This book does not seek to provide definitive answers but rather to provoke thought and encourage reflection. Each chapter delves into various aspects of contentment and growth—philosophical perspectives, psychological insights, societal implications, economic theories, and more. By exploring these themes, we hope to present a holistic view that encourages readers to see contentment and growth not as binaries, but as complementary parts of a fulfilling life.

Tanmeen Maken

CHAPTER

DEFINITIONS AND DISTINCTIONS—UNDERSTANDING THE BUILDING BLOCKS OF CONTENTMENT AND GROWTH

01

1.1 INTRODUCTION: DEFINING THE CORE CONCEPTS

Before delving into the complexities of contentment and growth, it's essential to clarify what these terms mean and how they differ. While both concepts are deeply intricately bound in human experience, they have distinct definitions and connotations that shape how we perceive and pursue them. This chapter lays the foundation by defining key terms—contentment, satisfaction, progress, and growth—and exploring their nuances.

By understanding the definitions and distinctions, we gain a clearer perspective on why these concepts often appear in opposition and how they can be reconciled in the pursuit of a balanced life.

1.2 WHAT IS CONTENTMENT? EXPLORING THE STATE OF INNER PEACE

Contentment is often described as a state of being satisfied and at peace with one's current circumstances. It involves accepting what one has without feeling the need for constant change or improvement. Contentment is associated with feelings of gratitude, tranquility, and fulfillment.

The Difference Between Contentment and Satisfaction

While contentment and satisfaction are sometimes used interchangeably, they are not synonymous. Satisfaction is often tied to the fulfillment of specific desires or needs. For example, one might feel satisfied after completing a project, receiving a reward, or achieving a particular goal. Satisfaction tends to be temporary and situation-specific, whereas contentment is a more enduring state that does not rely on external outcomes.

In this sense, contentment can be seen as a broader, more stable form of satisfaction that is not contingent on achieving specific objectives. It is less about 'having enough' and more about 'being enough'.

The Psychological and Emotional Benefits of Contentment

Research in positive psychology suggests that contentment is linked to greater overall well-being, lower stress levels, and improved mental health. People who experience contentment regularly are less likely to engage in social comparison and more likely to maintain positive relationships. The sense of inner peace that accompanies contentment allows individuals to approach challenges with equanimity and resilience.

However, contentment also poses a paradox: Can we be content and still strive for more? This question forms the crux of the tension between contentment and growth, as contentment can sometimes be perceived as a lack of ambition or motivation.

1.3 DEFINING GROWTH: THE DRIVE FOR IMPROVEMENT AND ACHIEVEMENT

Growth is often associated with progress, development, and the pursuit of new possibilities. It involves expanding one's skills, knowledge, and experiences and pushing beyond comfort zones to achieve greater heights. Growth is a dynamic and ongoing process that requires effort, resilience, and a willingness to embrace change.

Different Types of Growth: Personal, Societal, and Technological

1. **Personal Growth**: Personal growth encompasses the development of one's character, mindset, and abilities. It involves setting goals, overcoming obstacles, and striving for self-improvement. Personal growth is often motivated by a desire to become the best version of oneself.
2. **Societal Growth**: Societal growth refers to the advancement of social systems, including economic development, technological innovation, and social reforms. It is often measured by metrics such as GDP, employment rates, and educational attainment. Societal growth aims to improve the quality of life for communities and nations.
3. **Technological Growth**: Technological growth involves the creation and adoption of new technologies that enhance human capabilities and solve complex problems. It has transformed industries, communication, and daily life, contributing to economic prosperity and global interconnectedness.

Each type of growth has its own goals, measures of success, and potential challenges. While growth can lead to remarkable achievements and progress, it can also create tension with the desire for contentment.

The Dangers of Pursuing Growth at All Costs

While growth is often celebrated as a sign of success and progress, an unrelenting focus on growth can have negative consequences. Pursuing growth without consideration for well-being, ethics, or sustainability can lead to burnout, anxiety, and even societal harm. For example, economic growth driven by exploitation or environmental degradation can result in social inequality and ecological crises.

Therefore, the challenge lies in pursuing growth that is sustainable, ethical, and aligned with long-term well-being, both personally and collectively.

1.4 EXPLORING THE NUANCES: THE INTERPLAY BETWEEN CONTENTMENT AND GROWTH

The relationship between contentment and growth is not a simple binary. Rather, it is a dynamic interplay that varies across different contexts and stages of life. Understanding this interplay requires examining how contentment and growth influence each other and how they can be balanced.

Contentment as a Foundation for Growth

Contentment can serve as a stable foundation for growth by providing a sense of security and inner peace. When individuals feel content, they are less likely to be driven by fear or desperation. This allows them to pursue growth from a place of curiosity and purpose, rather than from a sense of lack or inadequacy.

For example, a person who is content with their current job may still seek new skills or experiences, not because they are dissatisfied, but because they enjoy learning and want to expand their horizons. In this way, contentment can coexist with a desire for growth, fostering a healthy and balanced approach to self-improvement.

The Role of Discontent in Motivating Growth

Discontent, on the other hand, can be a powerful motivator for growth. Feelings of dissatisfaction or frustration often signal areas of life where change is needed. Discontent can push individuals to leave unfulfilling situations, seek new opportunities, or challenge themselves to overcome obstacles.

However, it is important to distinguish between constructive discontent that leads to positive change and destructive discontent that results in perpetual dissatisfaction. The key is to harness discontent as a catalyst for growth while avoiding the trap of chronic dissatisfaction that prevents one from experiencing contentment.

1.5 THE DUAL NATURE OF PROGRESS: BALANCING CONTENTMENT AND GROWTH

Progress is often viewed as synonymous with growth, but it can also involve finding contentment in the present-moment. For some, progress means achieving tangible milestones, such as career advancement or financial success. For others, it means cultivating a deeper sense of inner peace and acceptance.

The Concept of 'Enough' in the Context of Growth

The idea of 'enough' is central to balancing contentment and growth. How do we determine when we have achieved enough growth or made enough progress? The concept of 'enough' varies for each person, depending on their values, goals, and circumstances.

For example, a person may decide that they have reached 'enough' in terms of career advancement when they achieve a role that allows them to work with purpose and maintain a healthy work-life balance. At this point, they may shift their focus from professional growth to personal or spiritual development.

Understanding and defining 'enough' allows individuals to pursue growth without falling into the trap of endless striving. It creates space for contentment to emerge alongside ambition.

1.6 CONCLUSION: SETTING THE STAGE FOR EXPLORATION

This chapter has laid the groundwork for understanding the complex relationship between contentment and growth. By defining key terms and exploring their nuances, we have established a foundation for deeper exploration in the chapters to come. As we continue this journey, we will examine the philosophical, psychological, and sociological dimensions of contentment and growth, providing insights into how these concepts shape our lives and experiences.

The stage is set for a thought-provoking journey through the paradox of contentment and growth. Let us delve deeper into this exploration, seeking to understand how we can achieve a balance that honors both our desire for progress and our need for inner peace.

CHAPTER

PHILOSOPHICAL PERSPECTIVES—EXPLORING ANCIENT AND MODERN VIEWS ON CONTENTMENT AND GROWTH

02

2.1 INTRODUCTION: THE PHILOSOPHICAL FOUNDATIONS OF CONTENTMENT AND GROWTH

Philosophy offers profound insights into the nature of contentment and growth, challenging us to think deeply about what it means to live a good life. Throughout history, philosophers have grappled with questions such as: Should we be content with what we have, or should we constantly strive for more? Can true happiness be found in the pursuit of growth, or does it reside in acceptance of the present?

This chapter examines various philosophical perspectives on contentment and growth, ranging from ancient teachings in Stoicism and Buddhism to modern existentialist viewpoints. By exploring these diverse perspectives, we gain a richer understanding of the complexities surrounding these concepts and their implications for our lives.

2.2 ANCIENT PHILOSOPHICAL VIEWS: CONTENTMENT AS A PATH TO WISDOM

Ancient philosophies often emphasize the importance of contentment as a means of achieving wisdom and inner peace. These teachings suggest that contentment arises not from external circumstances but from cultivating the right mindset and attitudes toward life.

Stoicism: Embracing Contentment Through Acceptance

The stoic philosophers of ancient Greece and Rome, such as Epictetus, Seneca, and Marcus Aurelius, taught that true contentment is found by accepting life's events with equanimity and focusing on what is within our control. According to Stoicism, external events are beyond our control, and it is our perceptions and responses that determine our happiness. Stoicism encourages individuals to cultivate *apatheia*— a state of inner tranquility free from emotional disturbances caused by desires, fears, or external judgments. By accepting life's challenges and setbacks with a calm and rational mind, one can achieve a sense of contentment that is resilient to external changes.

Stoic Practices for Cultivating Contentment

- **Practicing Negative Visualization**: Reflect on the impermanence of life and imagine losing the things you value. This practice helps build appreciation for what you have and reduces attachment.
- **Focusing on What Is Within Your Control**: Distinguish between what you can and cannot control. Accept what is outside your control and focus your efforts on changing your internal responses and actions.
- **Embracing Voluntary Discomfort**: Engage in small acts of discomfort, such as fasting or physical challenges, to build resilience and reduce dependence on external comforts.

Through these practices, Stoicism offers a path to contentment that is grounded in acceptance and self-discipline, enabling individuals to find peace amidst the inevitable changes of life.

Buddhism: The Middle Way and the Cessation of Craving

Buddhism, one of the world's oldest spiritual traditions, provides a different but complementary view on contentment. Central to Buddhist philosophy is the concept of *Dukkha*—the suffering and dissatisfaction that arise from attachment and craving. According to the Buddha, the root cause of suffering is the mind's incessant craving for more, whether it be material possessions, status, or sensory pleasures.

The Buddha's teachings on the *Four Noble Truths* and the *Eightfold Path* offer a way to overcome suffering and achieve *Nirvana*—a state of liberation and ultimate contentment. The key is to follow the Middle Way, a balanced approach that avoids the extremes of self-indulgence and self-mortification.

Buddhist Practices for Cultivating Contentment

- **Mindfulness Meditation**: Practice mindfulness to observe thoughts and emotions without attachment or judgment. This helps reduce craving and fosters a sense of inner peace.
- **Cultivating Compassion**: Develop compassion for oneself and others, recognizing that all beings experience suffering. Compassion reduces selfish desires and promotes contentment.
- **Letting Go of Attachment**: Reflect on the impermanence of all things and practice non-attachment. By letting go of the need to control outcomes, one can achieve a state of acceptance and tranquility.

Buddhism suggests that true contentment is not found in acquiring more but in letting go of desires and accepting the present-moment as it is. This philosophy challenges the notion that growth is always necessary for fulfillment.

2.3 MODERN PHILOSOPHICAL THOUGHTS: THE INTERSECTION OF HAPPINESS AND PROGRESS

Modern philosophy introduces new perspectives on contentment and growth, often focusing on the individual's search for meaning and the complexities of human existence in a rapidly changing world.

Existentialism: Creating Meaning in a World Without Inherent Purpose

Existentialist philosophers, such as Jean-Paul Sartre, Albert Camus, and Friedrich Nietzsche, grappled with the question of how to find meaning and fulfillment in a world that lacks inherent purpose. Existentialism suggests that life is inherently absurd, and it is up to each individual to create their own meaning and values.

For existentialists, growth is not merely about achieving external success but about embracing one's freedom and responsibility to define oneself. Contentment, in this view, is achieved not by passively accepting one's circumstances but by actively engaging in the process of self-creation and authenticity.

Key Existentialist Concepts

- **Freedom and Responsibility**: Individuals are free to choose their actions, but with this freedom comes the responsibility to make meaningful choices that define who they are.
- **Authenticity**: Authenticity involves living in accordance with one's true self and values, rather than conforming to external expectations or societal norms.
- **The Absurd**: The recognition that life is without inherent meaning can lead to despair, but it can also be a source of liberation, as individuals are free to create their own purpose.

Existentialism challenges the notion of contentment as complacency, suggesting that true fulfillment is found in embracing life's uncertainties and creating one's own path.

Positive Psychology: Finding Happiness Through Growth and Self-Actualization

Positive psychology, a modern branch of psychology with philosophical underpinnings, explores what makes life worth living and how individuals can achieve happiness and fulfillment. Psychologists like Martin Seligman and Mihaly Csikszentmihalyi emphasize the importance of pursuing growth and self-actualization.

According to positive psychology, contentment is not the absence of growth but the presence of well-being across various dimensions, such as relationships, purpose, and personal development. The concept of *flourishing* describes a state where individuals experience both personal growth and life satisfaction.

Positive Psychology Practices for Balancing Growth and Contentment

- **Gratitude Exercises**: Regularly reflecting on what one is grateful for can enhance feelings of contentment while reducing the urge for more.
- **Setting Meaningful Goals**: Set goals that align with one's values and strengths, fostering a sense of purpose and motivation.
- **Engaging in Flow Activities**: Participate in activities that promote flow—a state of deep immersion and engagement. Flow activities contribute to both personal growth and satisfaction.

Positive psychology suggests that contentment and growth are not mutually exclusive but can coexist, creating a life of both achievement and inner peace.

2.4 PHILOSOPHICAL TENSIONS: CAN GROWTH AND CONTENTMENT COEXIST?

Philosophical perspectives highlight the tension between growth and contentment, presenting contrasting views on whether these concepts can coexist or are inherently at odds.

The Stoic and Buddhist View: Growth Within Contentment

For Stoics and Buddhists, growth is not about acquiring more or achieving external success but about cultivating inner virtues and wisdom. Growth in this context is seen as an inward journey of self-mastery, where contentment serves as both the foundation and the goal.

The Existentialist View: Contentment Through Growth

In contrast, existentialists argue that contentment cannot be achieved without growth. They view the pursuit of authenticity and self-creation as essential to achieving true fulfillment. Contentment, in this view, arises from embracing one's freedom and actively shaping one's life, even in the face of adversity.

Positive Psychology: The Integration of Growth and Contentment

Positive psychology bridges these perspectives by suggesting that contentment and growth can be integrated. Growth contributes to overall well-being, and contentment is found in the balance of achievement and acceptance.

2.5 CONCLUSION: PHILOSOPHICAL INSIGHTS FOR MODERN LIFE

Philosophy provides diverse and thought-provoking perspectives on contentment and growth. Ancient teachings emphasize acceptance and inner peace, while modern philosophies explore the complexities of meaning, purpose, and self-creation. Together, these perspectives offer valuable insights into how we can navigate the paradox of contentment and growth in our own lives.

By drawing from these philosophical teachings, we can approach contentment and growth not as opposing forces but as complementary aspects of a fulfilling life. As we move forward, let us consider how these insights can inform our personal journeys and contribute to a deeper understanding of what it means to be truly content and to truly grow.

CHAPTER

PSYCHOLOGICAL INSIGHTS—UNDERSTANDING THE DYNAMICS OF HUMAN FULFILLMENT AND GROWTH

03

3.1 INTRODUCTION: THE PSYCHOLOGICAL DIMENSIONS OF CONTENTMENT AND GROWTH

Psychology provides valuable insights into the complex interplay between contentment and growth. Our thoughts, emotions, and behaviors are all shaped by psychological processes that influence how we pursue goals and experience satisfaction. Understanding these processes helps us navigate the tension between striving for more and appreciating what we have.

This chapter delves into key psychological theories and concepts that shed light on the dynamics of contentment and growth. We will explore Maslow's Hierarchy of Needs, the hedonic treadmill, and the flow state, providing a deeper understanding of how our minds shape our experiences of satisfaction and ambition.

3.2 MASLOW'S HIERARCHY OF NEEDS: A FRAMEWORK FOR UNDERSTANDING MOTIVATION

One of the most influential psychological theories of motivation is Abraham Maslow's *Hierarchy of Needs*. This framework suggests that human needs are arranged in a hierarchical order, from basic physiological needs to higher-level psychological and self-fulfillment needs. Maslow's theory provides a roadmap for understanding why people pursue growth and what it takes to achieve lasting contentment.

The Five Levels of Maslow's Hierarchy of Needs

1. **Physiological Needs**: At the base of the hierarchy are physiological needs, such as food, water, shelter, and sleep. These are the most basic and essential requirements for survival. When these needs are not met, individuals are driven to satisfy them before seeking anything else.
2. **Safety Needs**: Once physiological needs are met, people seek safety and security. This includes physical safety, financial stability, and health. The desire for stability and protection from harm is a fundamental driver of human behavior.
3. **Love and Belonging Needs**: The third level of the hierarchy involves social needs, such as love, friendship, and a sense of belonging. Humans are inherently social creatures, and feeling connected to others is crucial for emotional well-being.
4. **Esteem Needs**: Esteem needs are divided into two categories: self-esteem and esteem from others. People seek to build confidence, competence, and a sense of achievement. They also desire recognition, respect, and status from their peers.
5. **Self-Actualization Needs:** At the top of the hierarchy is self-actualization, which involves realizing one's potential and striving to become the best version of oneself. Self-actualization is about pursuing personal growth, creativity, and meaning.

Moving Up the Hierarchy: The Role of Growth and Contentment

According to Maslow, individuals move up the hierarchy as their lower-level needs are met. For example, a person who has satisfied their physiological and safety needs may focus on building relationships and seeking esteem. Growth occurs as people ascend the hierarchy, pursuing higher-level needs that contribute to personal fulfillment.

However, the theory also suggests that contentment is possible at any level of the hierarchy, depending on how well one's current needs are met. A person may experience contentment at the level of love and belonging if they have strong social connections, even if they have not yet reached self-actualization.

Understanding the hierarchy helps us see that growth and contentment are not mutually exclusive. Contentment can serve as a foundation for growth, and growth can lead to deeper forms of contentment.

Revisiting Maslow's Hierarchy: New Interpretations

Recent interpretations of Maslow's hierarchy suggest that the levels are not as rigid as originally proposed. People may pursue self-actualization even when their lower-level needs are not fully met. For example, individuals living in difficult circumstances may still seek personal growth and meaning through artistic expression or spiritual practices.

These nuances highlight that growth and contentment are complex and context-dependent. They cannot be understood through a one-size-fits-all model but require a consideration of individual circumstances and aspirations.

3.3 THE HEDONIC TREADMILL: WHY HAPPINESS IS OFTEN FLEETING

The *hedonic treadmill* is a psychological concept that explains why people tend to return to a baseline level of happiness, regardless of positive or negative life changes. It suggests that while achieving goals or acquiring new possessions may bring temporary joy, people quickly adapt to these changes, and their overall happiness levels remain relatively stable.

The Mechanism of the Hedonic Treadmill

The hedonic treadmill operates on the principle of *hedonic adaptation*. When something positive happens, such as a promotion or a new relationship, happiness levels temporarily rise. However, as people become accustomed to the new situation, the initial excitement fades, and their happiness returns to its previous baseline. The same process occurs with negative events—people may experience a dip in happiness, but over time, they adapt and return to their baseline level.

This phenomenon explains why people often feel the need to keep striving for more, even after achieving significant goals. The excitement of reaching a milestone or acquiring a new possession is short-lived, leading to a perpetual cycle of wanting and adapting.

Breaking Free from the Hedonic Treadmill

Understanding the hedonic treadmill can help individuals break free from the cycle of perpetual striving. One way to do this is to focus on experiences rather than material possessions. Research shows that people derive more lasting happiness from experiences, such as travel, learning, or spending time with loved ones, than from material goods.

Another strategy is to cultivate gratitude. Regularly reflecting on the things one is grateful for can counteract hedonic adaptation and increase long-term well-being. Gratitude shifts focus from what is lacking to what is already present, fostering a sense of contentment.

The hedonic treadmill reminds us that growth, when driven by external rewards, may not lead to lasting satisfaction. True fulfillment comes from finding value in the present-moment and pursuing growth for its own sake.

3.4 FLOW STATE: ACHIEVING OPTIMAL EXPERIENCE AND FULFILLMENT

The concept of *flow* was introduced by psychologist Mihaly Csikszentmihalyi to describe a state of complete immersion and enjoyment in an activity. When people are in a flow state, they experience deep focus, a sense of control, and intrinsic satisfaction. Flow is often referred to as being 'in the zone', where the challenges of the activity match one's skills, creating an optimal experience.

The Characteristics of Flow

Flow is characterized by the following elements:

1. **Clear Goals and Immediate Feedback**: People in a flow state have clear objectives and receive immediate feedback on their progress. This keeps them engaged and motivated.
2. **Balance Between Challenge and Skill**: Flow occurs when the difficulty of the task is slightly above one's skill level. This balance prevents boredom and anxiety, creating a sense of mastery and enjoyment.
3. **Loss of Self-Consciousness**: People in a flow state are so absorbed in the activity that they lose awareness of themselves and their surroundings. Time seems to fly by, and distractions fade away.

Flow is closely linked to both contentment and growth. It fosters a sense of fulfillment in the present-moment while promoting skill development and personal growth. People who frequently experience flow report higher levels of happiness and well-being.

Cultivating Flow in Daily Life

Flow can be cultivated in various activities, from professional work to hobbies like sports, art, or gardening. To experience flow more often, individuals can:

- Choose activities that match their skills and push them slightly beyond their comfort zone.
- Set clear, achievable goals for the task at hand.
- Minimize distractions and create an environment conducive to deep focus.

By integrating flow into everyday life, individuals can find a sense of contentment and growth in even the simplest activities.

3.5 PSYCHOLOGICAL STRATEGIES FOR BALANCING GROWTH AND CONTENTMENT

Research in positive psychology provides practical strategies for balancing the pursuit of growth with the experience of contentment. These strategies include developing a growth mindset, practicing self-compassion, and engaging in mindful goal-setting.

Developing a Growth Mindset

A growth mindset, as defined by psychologist Carol Dweck, involves believing that abilities and intelligence can be developed through effort and learning. This mindset encourages resilience and persistence, promoting a healthy approach to growth. People with a growth mindset see challenges as opportunities for learning and view failures as temporary setbacks.

Practicing Self-Compassion

Self-compassion involves treating oneself with kindness and understanding, especially during setbacks or failures. People who practice self-compassion are less likely to experience burnout or chronic dissatisfaction, as they are better able to cope with challenges and maintain a sense of inner peace.

Engaging in Mindful Goal-Setting

Mindful goal-setting involves choosing goals that are meaningful and aligned with one's values. This approach ensures that the pursuit of growth contributes to overall well-being, rather than leading to burnout or discontent.

By integrating these strategies into daily life, individuals can create a balance that supports both personal development and lasting contentment.

3.6 CONCLUSION: A PSYCHOLOGICAL PERSPECTIVE ON GROWTH AND CONTENTMENT

Psychology provides valuable insights into why contentment and growth often seem at odds and how we can harmonize them. From understanding human motivation through Maslow's Hierarchy of Needs to recognizing the influence of the hedonic treadmill and the power of flow, psychological theories shed light on our pursuit of fulfillment.

By applying these insights and strategies, we can create a more balanced approach to personal growth—one that fosters deep contentment and meaningful development. As we move forward in this exploration, the psychological principles discussed in this chapter will serve as a foundation for understanding how our minds shape our experiences of contentment and growth.

CHAPTER

SOCIOLOGICAL ASPECTS—HOW SOCIETY SHAPES OUR PERCEPTION OF CONTENTMENT AND GROWTH

04

4.1 INTRODUCTION: THE INFLUENCE OF SOCIETY ON INDIVIDUAL PERCEPTIONS

Our understanding of contentment and growth is not formed in isolation—it is deeply influenced by the social context in which we live. Cultural values, societal expectations, and economic structures all play a role in shaping our desires, motivations, and definitions of success. What one society considers a sign of success may be seen as an excessive pursuit in another. Similarly, the way we experience contentment can be influenced by societal norms and social comparisons.

This chapter explores the sociological dimensions of contentment and growth, examining how different societies and cultures perceive these concepts. We'll delve into the impact of cultural values, societal expectations, and social comparison, providing insights into how our social environment shapes our personal aspirations and sense of fulfillment.

4.2 CULTURAL DIFFERENCES IN PERCEIVING CONTENTMENT AND GROWTH

Different cultures have distinct attitudes toward contentment and growth. These cultural differences influence how people set goals, measure success, and experience fulfillment. Understanding these cultural nuances helps explain why contentment and growth can look very different depending on where one is in the world.

Individualistic vs. Collectivistic Cultures

One of the primary distinctions in cultural attitudes toward contentment and growth is the difference between individualistic and collectivistic cultures.

1. **Individualistic Cultures**: In individualistic cultures, such as those in the United States, Canada, and many Western European countries, personal achievements and self-improvement are highly valued. People are encouraged to set personal goals, strive for career success, and prioritize individual autonomy. Growth is often defined in terms of personal advancement, such as promotions, financial success, or self-development.
2. **Collectivistic Cultures**: In collectivistic cultures, such as those in Japan, China, and many other Asian and African countries, the emphasis is on fulfilling one's role within the family and society. Contentment is often linked to social harmony and fulfilling collective responsibilities rather than personal achievement. Growth is viewed in the context of contributing to the well-being of the community and maintaining social cohesion.

These cultural distinctions shape how individuals approach contentment and growth. For example, a person in an individualistic culture may feel pressured to constantly pursue new goals and achievements, while a person in a collectivistic culture may prioritize stability and relational harmony over personal success.

Cultural Values and the Pursuit of Happiness

Cultural values play a significant role in defining what it means to be happy and fulfilled. For instance, cultures that value material success and individual achievement may emphasize growth through career advancement and financial wealth. In contrast, cultures that value spirituality, community, or simplicity may promote contentment through mindfulness, gratitude, and social relationships.

Examples of Cultural Differences in Defining Happiness

- In Bhutan, the concept of *Gross National Happiness* (GNH) is prioritized over Gross Domestic Product (GDP), reflecting the country's focus on well-being and spiritual contentment rather than material wealth.

- In Scandinavian countries like Denmark and Sweden, social policies and cultural norms emphasize *hygge* (a sense of coziness and contentment) and *lagom* (moderation and balance), promoting a lifestyle of simplicity and satisfaction with what one has.

Understanding these cultural differences provides a broader perspective on how contentment and growth are experienced and pursued around the world.

4.3 THE IMPACT OF SOCIETAL EXPECTATIONS ON INDIVIDUAL SATISFACTION

Societal expectations exert a powerful influence on how we perceive our own contentment and growth. From a young age, we are socialized to internalize messages about what it means to be successful, happy, and fulfilled. These messages often come from parents, educators, peers, and the media, shaping our beliefs about what we should strive for and how we should measure our worth.

Social Norms and the Pressure to Conform

Social norms define what is considered desirable or acceptable in a given society. For example, in many Western countries, there is a strong emphasis on financial success, professional advancement, and material wealth. People who do not conform to these standards may feel pressured to pursue careers or lifestyles that do not align with their true desires, leading to a disconnection between their goals and their sense of contentment.

In contrast, societies that value humility, simplicity, or spiritual development may discourage displays of wealth or overt ambition. In such societies, individuals may experience contentment through aligning with social expectations of modesty and community service rather than pursuing personal achievements.

The Role of Socialization in Shaping Aspirations

Socialization is the process by which individuals learn and internalize the values, norms, and expectations of their society. This process begins in childhood and continues throughout life, influencing our choices and aspirations.

Examples of Socialization Influencing Aspirations

- In families where academic success is highly valued, children may feel pressure to excel in school and pursue prestigious careers, even if their true passions lie elsewhere.
- In communities where volunteer work and social responsibility are emphasized, individuals may prioritize contributing to social causes over pursuing personal wealth or status.

Societal expectations can both inspire and constrain our pursuit of growth and contentment. Understanding these influences helps us recognize when our goals are shaped by external pressures rather than intrinsic desires.

4.4 THE ROLE OF SOCIAL COMPARISON IN SHAPING CONTENTMENT AND GROWTH

Social comparison is a powerful force that shapes how we perceive contentment and growth. People naturally compare themselves to others, using these comparisons as a benchmark for their own success and happiness. While social comparison can motivate individuals to improve, it can also lead to envy, dissatisfaction, and a constant feeling of inadequacy.

The Social Comparison Theory

Social comparison theory, developed by psychologist Leon Festinger, suggests that people evaluate their own abilities and achievements by comparing themselves to others. There are two types of social comparisons:

1. **Upward Comparison**: Comparing oneself to someone perceived as better off. This can lead to feelings of inadequacy and discontent, but it can also serve as motivation for personal growth.
2. **Downward Comparison**: Comparing oneself to someone perceived as worse off. This can enhance self-esteem and contentment but may also foster complacency.

The rise of social media has amplified the impact of social comparison. People are constantly exposed to curated images of others' successes and lifestyles, creating a skewed perception of reality where everyone else seems happier, more successful, or more fulfilled.

Mitigating the Negative Effects of Social Comparison

To mitigate the negative effects of social comparison, it's essential to develop self-awareness and focus on personal goals that align with one's values and aspirations. Strategies for managing social comparison include:

- **Limiting Social Media Exposure**: Reducing time spent on social media can decrease exposure to unrealistic comparisons and improve overall well-being.
- **Practicing Gratitude**: Regularly reflecting on what one is grateful for shifts focus away from what others have and fosters a sense of contentment.
- **Setting Personal Benchmarks**: Define success and growth based on personal values and goals rather than external comparisons.

By understanding the dynamics of social comparison, individuals can navigate the pressure to keep up with others and cultivate a more authentic sense of contentment and growth.

4.5 SOCIOECONOMIC FACTORS AND THE EXPERIENCE OF CONTENTMENT AND GROWTH

Socioeconomic factors such as income, education, and employment play a significant role in shaping how individuals experience contentment and growth. People in different socioeconomic positions face varying opportunities and challenges that influence their ability to pursue growth and achieve satisfaction.

Economic Inequality and Its Impact on Contentment

Economic inequality is a major barrier to contentment and growth for many individuals. In societies with high levels of inequality, people in lower socioeconomic positions often face additional stressors, such as job insecurity, poor health outcomes, and limited access to resources. These stressors impede their ability to focus on personal development and contribute to a sense of powerlessness.

Conversely, those in higher socioeconomic positions may have more opportunities for growth but may also experience pressures to maintain their status, leading to a different set of challenges in achieving contentment.

The Role of Education and Employment in Shaping Aspirations

Education and employment are key factors in determining an individual's capacity for growth and fulfillment. Access to quality education opens doors to better job opportunities, higher income, and greater life satisfaction. Employment, particularly in fulfilling and meaningful work, contributes to a sense of purpose and personal growth.

Socioeconomic factors can either support or hinder an individual's pursuit of growth and contentment, highlighting the need for policies that promote equity and create opportunities for all members of society.

4.6 CONCLUSION: THE SOCIOLOGICAL CONTEXT OF CONTENTMENT AND GROWTH

Our understanding of contentment and growth is shaped not only by personal desires but also by the social environment in which we live. Societal norms, cultural values, and socioeconomic factors all influence how we define success, what we consider fulfilling, and how we pursue our goals.

The journey to achieving a balance between contentment and growth is not just an internal one. It is shaped by the cultural narratives we inherit, the societal roles we play, and the institutional structures we navigate. Understanding these sociological influences allows us to critically evaluate our own goals and redefine what it means to lead a fulfilling life in the context of the society we inhabit.

CHAPTER

ECONOMIC CONSIDERATIONS—THE INTERPLAY BETWEEN ECONOMIC GROWTH AND HUMAN SATISFACTION

05

5.1 INTRODUCTION: THE ECONOMICS OF CONTENTMENT AND GROWTH

Economics plays a significant role in shaping our understanding of contentment and growth. The pursuit of economic growth is often seen as synonymous with progress and prosperity, yet it does not always translate into higher levels of happiness and well-being. Economic policies and models prioritize growth in Gross Domestic Product (GDP), employment rates, and productivity, but they sometimes overlook the human factors that contribute to overall satisfaction and quality of life.

This chapter delves into the economic considerations of contentment and growth, examining how economic growth models influence our perceptions of success, the relationship between wealth and happiness, and alternative frameworks such as Gross National Happiness. By exploring these topics, we can gain a deeper understanding of how economics intersects with human fulfillment and the broader implications for society.

5.2 ECONOMIC GROWTH MODELS AND THEIR ASSUMPTIONS ABOUT HUMAN SATISFACTION

Traditional economic growth models are primarily concerned with increasing the output of goods and services within a country. Growth is measured by metrics such as GDP, productivity, and investment, with the assumption that higher levels of economic activity lead to improved living standards and greater well-being. However, this focus on economic growth can sometimes mask underlying issues related to inequality, resource distribution, and social well-being.

The GDP Measure and Its Limitations

GDP, the most commonly used measure of economic growth, calculates the total value of goods and services produced within a country over a specified period. While GDP growth is often associated with higher employment and income levels, it does not capture the distribution of wealth, environmental sustainability, or the quality of life.

For example, a country could experience GDP growth while a significant portion of its population remains in poverty. Moreover, activities that deplete natural resources or contribute to pollution can increase GDP in the short-term but lead to long-term negative impacts on well-being.

This narrow focus on GDP has led to calls for alternative measures that better capture the multidimensional nature of human satisfaction and societal progress.

The Easterlin Paradox: Does Economic Growth Lead to Greater Happiness?

The *Easterlin Paradox*, named after economist Richard Easterlin, challenges the assumption that higher income levels always lead to greater happiness. According to the paradox, while happiness tends to increase with income up to a certain point, beyond a certain threshold, further increases in income have a diminishing impact on well-being.

This phenomenon is observed both within and across countries. For example, people in wealthy countries such as the United States report higher levels of happiness compared to those in low-income countries, but within wealthy countries, higher income levels do not necessarily lead to higher life satisfaction.

The Easterlin Paradox suggests that once basic needs are met, factors such as social relationships, personal fulfillment, and mental health become more important determinants of happiness than additional income. This insight has significant implications for how we think about economic growth and its role in promoting human well-being.

5.3 CONCEPTS LIKE GROSS NATIONAL HAPPINESS: RETHINKING PROGRESS AND DEVELOPMENT

In response to the limitations of GDP as a measure of progress, some countries and organizations have adopted alternative frameworks that prioritize well-being, sustainability, and social equity. One such framework is *Gross National Happiness* (GNH), which was developed in Bhutan as a holistic approach to development.

Gross National Happiness: A Holistic Measure of Well-Being

Gross National Happiness (GNH) measures societal progress based on four pillars:

1. **Sustainable and Equitable Socioeconomic Development**: GNH emphasizes economic growth that is inclusive and benefits all members of society. It seeks to reduce inequality and ensure that economic development does not come at the expense of environmental sustainability or social harmony.
2. **Preservation and Promotion of Culture**: GNH values cultural preservation and the promotion of traditional values, recognizing that cultural heritage contributes to a sense of identity and community.
3. **Conservation of the Environment**: Environmental sustainability is a key component of GNH. It encourages responsible resource management and the protection of natural ecosystems.
4. **Good Governance**: GNH emphasizes transparent and accountable governance that prioritizes the well-being of citizens and fosters trust in institutions.

These pillars are further divided into nine domains, including psychological well-being, health, education, and time use, which together provide a comprehensive picture of human fulfillment.

Bhutan's adoption of GNH has gained international attention and inspired other countries to consider alternative measures of progress that go beyond GDP.

While GNH is not without its challenges, it offers a valuable model for integrating economic, social, and environmental considerations into development policies.

Other Alternative Measures: Human Development Index and Well-being Economy

Other frameworks, such as the *Human Development Index (HDI)* and the *Well-being Economy*, also emphasize human-centric measures of progress. HDI combines indicators of health, education, and income to provide a broader measure of development, while the Well-being Economy seeks to align economic activities with environmental sustainability and social equity.

These alternative frameworks challenge the traditional focus on economic growth and highlight the need for policies that promote holistic well-being.

5.4 CONSUMERISM AND ITS RELATIONSHIP TO CONTENTMENT

Consumerism, or the continual acquisition of goods and services, is often linked to the pursuit of contentment and happiness in modern societies. Advertisements and social norms promote the idea that buying more leads to greater satisfaction. However, research shows that excessive consumerism can lead to diminished well-being and environmental harm.

The Psychology of Consumerism

Consumerism is driven by the belief that material possessions can enhance happiness and status. Marketers and advertisers exploit this belief by creating desires for new products and services, often by appealing to emotions such as fear, envy, or a desire for social acceptance.

While purchasing new items can provide a temporary boost in happiness, the effect is usually short-lived due to hedonic adaptation – the tendency to quickly return to a baseline level of satisfaction. This creates a cycle where people continuously seek new possessions to maintain the initial sense of joy, leading to overconsumption and financial stress.

The Impact of Consumerism on Well-being and the Environment

Excessive consumerism can negatively impact both personal well-being and the environment. On a personal level, it can lead to financial insecurity, stress, and dissatisfaction. On a societal level, consumerism drives the depletion of natural resources, contributes to pollution, and exacerbates climate change.

Breaking free from the cycle of consumerism involves redefining what it means to be content. Practices such as minimalism, mindful consumption, and focusing on experiences over possessions can promote a more sustainable and fulfilling lifestyle.

5.5 THE ECONOMIC IMPACT OF CONTENTMENT: HOW HAPPINESS INFLUENCES ECONOMIC GROWTH

While economic growth can influence contentment, the reverse is also true—contentment and happiness can impact economic performance. Research suggests that happier individuals are more productive, engaged, and creative, leading to better outcomes for businesses and economies.

Happiness and Productivity

Happier employees tend to be more motivated, perform better, and show greater loyalty to their organizations. This has led some companies to prioritize employee well-being through initiatives such as flexible work arrangements, mental health support, and opportunities for personal growth.

In countries where overall happiness levels are high, economic growth can benefit from a more engaged and innovative workforce. This creates a positive feedback loop where happiness and economic success reinforce each other.

The Role of Public Policy in Promoting Happiness

Governments can play a role in promoting contentment and well-being through policies that address social determinants of happiness, such as healthcare, education, and social safety nets. By creating conditions that support well-being, policymakers can contribute to both individual satisfaction and economic prosperity.

5.6 BALANCING ECONOMIC GROWTH WITH HUMAN FULFILLMENT

The challenge lies in balancing economic growth with human fulfillment. While economic development is essential for reducing poverty and improving living standards, it should not come at the cost of well-being, social equity, or environmental sustainability.

Strategies for Achieving Balance

1. **Implementing Progressive Economic Policies**: Policies that promote equitable wealth distribution, environmental protection, and social welfare can help align economic growth with human fulfillment.
2. **Promoting Corporate Social Responsibility (CSR)**: Encouraging businesses to adopt CSR practices that prioritize employee well-being, ethical conduct, and community engagement can foster a more sustainable and humane economy.
3. **Supporting Sustainable Consumption and Production**: Shifting toward sustainable consumption and production practices can reduce environmental impact and promote long-term well-being.

Achieving this balance requires a shift in priorities—from a narrow focus on economic metrics to a broader perspective that values human and environmental health.

5.7 CONCLUSION: RETHINKING ECONOMIC SUCCESS

Economic considerations are crucial for understanding the relationship between contentment and growth. Traditional growth models prioritize GDP and productivity, but they often overlook the human and environmental costs of relentless economic expansion. Alternative frameworks such as Gross National Happiness and the Well-Being Economy offer more holistic measures of progress that prioritize human fulfillment and sustainability.

By rethinking economic success, we can create a world where growth and contentment are not in conflict but are complementary aspects of a prosperous and fulfilling society. As we continue to explore the complexities of contentment and growth, the economic perspective provides valuable insights into how we can pursue prosperity that truly enhances the quality of life for all.

CHAPTER

BIOLOGICAL AND EVOLUTIONARY PERSPECTIVES—THE ROLE OF HUMAN NATURE IN THE PURSUIT OF CONTENTMENT AND GROWTH

06

6.1 INTRODUCTION: THE BIOLOGICAL ROOTS OF HUMAN BEHAVIOR

Understanding contentment and growth requires examining their roots in human biology and evolution. Our behaviors, emotions, and desires are not merely shaped by culture or personal experiences; they are also influenced by our biological makeup and evolutionary history. The drive for growth and the capacity for contentment have both played crucial roles in human survival and development, guiding our responses to the environment and our interactions with others.

This chapter explores the biological and evolutionary foundations of contentment and growth. We'll delve into the role of brain chemistry, the evolutionary advantages of striving, and the brain's capacity for change and development. By examining these factors, we can gain a deeper understanding of why the tension between contentment and growth exists and how it has shaped human behavior over millennia.

6.2 THE ROLE OF DOPAMINE IN REWARD AND SATISFACTION

Dopamine, a neurotransmitter in the brain, is often called the 'feel-good' chemical because of its role in regulating pleasure, reward, and motivation. It plays a central role in the brain's reward system, influencing how we experience satisfaction and how we pursue goals.

Dopamine and the Pursuit of Growth

Dopamine is released when we anticipate or achieve a rewarding outcome, such as completing a task, acquiring a new skill, or receiving praise. This release creates feelings of pleasure and reinforces behaviors that lead to rewards. In this sense, dopamine drives us to seek out new experiences, set goals, and strive for growth.

However, the pursuit of growth can become problematic when it is fueled by a constant desire for dopamine-induced pleasure. The brain's reward system is designed to seek novelty and challenge, which can lead to a perpetual cycle of wanting more. This is why people often feel compelled to set new goals as soon as they achieve previous ones, making it difficult to experience lasting contentment.

Dopamine's Role in Learning and Adaptation: Dopamine is not just associated with pleasure but also with learning. It helps the brain form associations between behaviors and rewards, making it a key player in habit formation. When a behavior consistently leads to a positive outcome, dopamine strengthens the neural pathways associated with that behavior, making it more likely to be repeated in the future.

Understanding dopamine's role in reward and motivation helps explain why people often feel driven to pursue growth even after achieving significant milestones. It also highlights the need to balance the pursuit of new goals with practices that promote lasting contentment, such as mindfulness and gratitude.

Dopamine and the Hedonic Treadmill

The concept of the *hedonic treadmill*, introduced in Chapter 3, is closely linked to dopamine. When people experience positive events, such as a promotion or a new relationship, dopamine levels rise, leading to a temporary boost in happiness. However, as people adapt to these changes, their dopamine levels return to baseline, and the initial pleasure fades. This creates a cycle where people seek out new rewards to maintain the feeling of pleasure, contributing to the hedonic treadmill effect.

Breaking free from this cycle requires focusing on non-dopaminergic sources of contentment, such as cultivating meaningful relationships, practicing self-acceptance, and engaging in activities that promote intrinsic satisfaction.

6.3 EVOLUTIONARY ADVANTAGES OF PERPETUAL STRIVING

The drive for growth and achievement has deep evolutionary roots. Throughout human history, the ability to strive for more—whether it be food, shelter, or social status—has been linked to survival and reproductive success. This evolutionary perspective helps explain why humans are wired to seek out challenges and push beyond their current limits.

The Evolutionary Basis of Ambition

Early humans who were driven to explore new territories, innovate with tools, and acquire resources were more likely to survive and pass on their genes. This drive for growth and improvement was not just about personal gain—it also benefited the group by ensuring access to resources and enhancing social cohesion.

The desire for status and recognition also has evolutionary underpinnings. In many social species, including humans, individuals who achieve higher social status have better access to resources, mating opportunities, and social support. This has led to the development of behaviors and traits that promote competitiveness, ambition, and goal-setting.

While these traits have contributed to human success, they can also lead to perpetual striving and dissatisfaction in modern contexts where survival is no longer at stake. Understanding the evolutionary roots of ambition helps us recognize the sources of our desires and the challenges of finding contentment in a world of abundance.

The Role of Competition and Cooperation

Human evolution has been shaped by both competition and cooperation. While competition drives individuals to strive for more, cooperation fosters social bonds and collective well-being. The interplay between these two forces has influenced how humans pursue growth and experience contentment.

For example, in hunter-gatherer societies, individuals competed for resources and social status, but they also cooperated to hunt, share food, and protect one another. This balance between competition and cooperation created a social environment where growth was linked to the well-being of the entire group, not just the individual.

In modern societies, the emphasis on individual achievement and competition can sometimes undermine social cohesion and contentment. Reconnecting with the cooperative aspects of human nature—such as community building, altruism, and mutual support—can help balance the drive for personal growth with a sense of collective contentment.

6.4 NEUROPLASTICITY AND THE BRAIN'S CAPACITY FOR GROWTH

The human brain has an extraordinary capacity for growth and adaptation, a phenomenon known as *neuroplasticity*. Neuroplasticity refers to the brain's ability to reorganize itself by forming new neural connections throughout life. This capacity for change allows people to learn new skills, recover from injuries, and adapt to new environments.

The Role of Neuroplasticity in Personal Development

Neuroplasticity enables individuals to grow in response to experiences, practice, and learning. When people engage in new activities, such as learning a language or practicing a sport, the brain forms new neural pathways that strengthen over time. This process underlies the development of new habits, skills, and behaviors.

Understanding neuroplasticity highlights the potential for continuous growth, regardless of age or previous experiences. It suggests that individuals have the capacity to change their thoughts, behaviors, and even their sense of identity through intentional practice and learning.

The Relationship Between Neuroplasticity and Contentment

While neuroplasticity supports personal growth, it also plays a role in shaping contentment. Practices such as mindfulness meditation have been shown to change the structure and function of the brain, enhancing areas associated with emotional regulation, self-awareness, and empathy. These changes promote a sense of inner peace and contentment, suggesting that the brain's capacity for growth can be harnessed to cultivate well-being as well as achievement.

Neuroplasticity reminds us that contentment is not a fixed state but one that can be developed through intentional practices. By cultivating positive habits and mindsets, individuals can rewire their brains to experience greater satisfaction and fulfillment.

6.5 THE BIOLOGICAL BALANCE: FINDING EQUILIBRIUM BETWEEN GROWTH AND CONTENTMENT

The biological and evolutionary perspectives on contentment and growth highlight the need for balance. While the drive for growth is rooted in our evolutionary history and supported by our brain chemistry, contentment is essential for mental health and overall well-being.

Balancing Dopamine and Serotonin

Dopamine is often associated with the pursuit of rewards, while serotonin is linked to feelings of contentment, well-being, and social bonding. Finding a balance between these two neurotransmitters is key to achieving equilibrium between growth and satisfaction.

Ways to Balance Dopamine and Serotonin

- **Engage in Physical Activity**: Exercise increases levels of both dopamine and serotonin, promoting a balance between motivation and relaxation.
- **Practice Mindfulness and Meditation**: Mindfulness practices reduce the overactivity of dopamine-driven behaviors and increase serotonin levels, enhancing contentment and peace.
- **Focus on Social Connections**: Social interactions, such as spending time with friends and family, boost serotonin levels, fostering a sense of belonging and contentment.

Embracing Evolutionary Drives While Cultivating Present-Moment Awareness

The evolutionary drive for growth and achievement does not have to be at odds with contentment. By recognizing these drives and consciously choosing how to respond to them, individuals can harness their innate desires for growth in ways that support well-being. Practices such as goal-setting, self-reflection, and mindfulness can help individuals navigate the tension between striving and being, leading to a more balanced life.

6.6 CONCLUSION: THE BIOLOGICAL AND EVOLUTIONARY FOUNDATIONS OF HUMAN FULFILLMENT

Biological and evolutionary perspectives provide valuable insights into the complex relationship between contentment and growth. From the role of dopamine in driving motivation to the evolutionary advantages of striving for more, these factors have shaped human behavior for thousands of years.

Understanding the biological roots of our desires and the brain's capacity for growth allows us to navigate the paradox of contentment and growth more effectively. By embracing our biological nature while cultivating practices that promote well-being, we can create a life that honors both the pursuit of achievement and the experience of deep contentment.

CHAPTER

HISTORICAL EXAMPLES—LESSONS FROM INDIVIDUALS AND SOCIETIES ON CONTENTMENT AND GROWTH

07

7.1 INTRODUCTION: LEARNING FROM HISTORY

History is filled with stories of individuals and societies that have grappled with the tension between contentment and growth. Some have thrived by achieving a balance, while others have struggled or even collapsed under the weight of relentless ambition or stagnation. Examining historical examples provides valuable lessons on how contentment and growth have been pursued, understood, and defined over time.

This chapter explores notable case studies of individuals and societies that have prioritized either contentment or growth—or have managed to balance both. By analyzing their successes, failures, and lasting impacts, we can gain insights into the timeless nature of this paradox and apply these lessons to our own lives and communities.

7.2 CASE STUDIES OF INDIVIDUALS: THE PURSUIT OF PERSONAL GROWTH AND INNER PEACE

Throughout history, many influential figures have grappled with the tension between contentment and growth, each finding their own path to fulfillment. Their stories illustrate the diverse ways in which individuals have navigated this complex relationship.

Case Study 1: Siddhartha Gautama (The Buddha)

Siddhartha Gautama, known as the Buddha, is one of the most profound examples of an individual who sought to reconcile growth and contentment. Born into wealth and luxury as a prince, Siddhartha experienced a life of indulgence before realizing that material wealth and sensual pleasures could not bring lasting happiness.

Determined to understand the nature of suffering and achieve true contentment, he renounced his princely life and embarked on a spiritual journey. After years of ascetic practices and deep meditation, he attained enlightenment under the Bodhi tree, discovering the Middle Way – a path that avoids the extremes of self-indulgence and self-mortification.

Key Lessons from the Buddha's Life

- True contentment comes from within and cannot be found through external achievements or possessions.
- Growth is a process of inner transformation and self-mastery rather than the accumulation of wealth or status.
- Finding balance between desires and acceptance is essential for lasting peace.

The Buddha's teachings continue to inspire millions around the world, offering a timeless model of contentment and growth through spiritual development and self-understanding.

Case Study 2: Leonardo da Vinci—The Relentless Pursuit of Knowledge

Leonardo da Vinci, the quintessential Renaissance man, exemplifies the relentless pursuit of growth and mastery. As a polymath, Leonardo explored a wide range of fields, including painting, anatomy, engineering, and astronomy. His insatiable curiosity and drive for knowledge led him to create some of the most iconic artworks and scientific studies in history.

However, Leonardo's quest for growth came at a personal cost. He struggled with self-doubt and perfectionism, often leaving projects unfinished in his pursuit of ever-deeper understanding. Despite these challenges, his dedication to growth resulted in groundbreaking achievements that have influenced generations of thinkers and creators.

Key Lessons from Leonardo da Vinci's Life

- The pursuit of growth can lead to extraordinary achievements but must be balanced with self-acceptance to prevent burnout and frustration.
- Curiosity and the desire for knowledge are powerful motivators for growth, but they can also create a sense of never-ending striving.
- Finding contentment in the process of exploration and learning, rather than in the completion of specific goals, can help reconcile growth with fulfillment.

Leonardo's life serves as a testament to the power of curiosity and the importance of balancing ambition with self-compassion.

Case Study 3: Mahatma Gandhi—Growth Through Ethical Living and Social Change

Mahatma Gandhi's life and philosophy embody the integration of growth and contentment through ethical living and social activism. Gandhi's concept of *Swaraj* (self-rule) emphasized personal growth through self-discipline, ethical conduct, and nonviolent resistance. He sought to achieve both personal and societal transformation by adhering to principles such as *ahimsa* (nonviolence) and *satya* (truth).

Gandhi's emphasis on simplicity and self-restraint was a form of contentment rooted in the rejection of materialism and the pursuit of inner peace. At the same time, his dedication to social and political change through nonviolent resistance demonstrated a commitment to growth that extended beyond the self to the collective well-being of society.

Key Lessons from Gandhi's Life

- Growth and contentment can be achieved through ethical living and a commitment to social justice.
- Personal growth is not just about self-improvement but also about contributing to the betterment of society.
- Contentment can be cultivated through simplicity and self-discipline, even in the face of external challenges.

Gandhi's legacy continues to inspire movements for social justice and nonviolent resistance, highlighting the possibility of achieving growth and contentment through principled action.

7.3 HISTORICAL SOCIETIES: THE RISE AND FALL OF CIVILIZATIONS

The history of civilizations provides rich examples of how societies have navigated the balance between growth and contentment. Some societies have flourished by prioritizing sustainability and well-being, while others have collapsed under the weight of unchecked expansion or complacency.

The Roman Empire: A Story of Ambition and Decline

The Roman Empire, one of the most powerful civilizations in history, experienced a meteoric rise fueled by military conquests, political ambition, and economic growth. Rome's expansion brought immense wealth, cultural exchange, and technological advancements, but it also created internal divisions, social inequality, and environmental degradation.

As the empire grew, so did the demands on its resources and the pressures on its political system. The pursuit of ever-greater power and wealth ultimately led to corruption, political instability, and the erosion of social cohesion. By the time of its fall, the empire had lost the ability to sustain its growth, leading to fragmentation and decline.

Key Lessons from the Roman Empire

- Unchecked growth, without consideration for social and environmental sustainability, can lead to internal decay and collapse.
- Societal success depends not only on economic and military power but also on social cohesion, ethical governance, and resource management.
- Finding balance between expansion and stability is essential for the long-term survival of a civilization.

The Roman Empire's rise and fall illustrate the dangers of pursuing growth at all costs and the importance of integrating contentment and sustainability into societal development.

The Inca Empire: A Model of Sustainable Growth and Social Harmony

In contrast to the Roman Empire, the Inca Empire in South America prioritized sustainable development and social welfare. The Incas implemented sophisticated agricultural techniques, such as terrace farming and irrigation systems, that allowed them to cultivate food in challenging environments. Their emphasis on communal labor and resource sharing created a strong sense of social cohesion and minimized inequality.

The Incas also respected the natural environment, viewing themselves as stewards of the land. This ecological consciousness enabled them to maintain a stable food supply and support a large population without depleting resources.

However, despite their focus on sustainability and social harmony, the Inca Empire was vulnerable to external threats. The arrival of the Spanish conquistadors led to the empire's rapid downfall, demonstrating that even societies that achieve internal balance can be disrupted by external forces.

Key Lessons from the Inca Empire

- Sustainable growth and social harmony are possible when societies prioritize environmental stewardship and community welfare.
- Societies must balance internal stability with the ability to adapt to external changes and threats.
- Contentment can be fostered through practices that promote collective well-being and environmental respect.

The Inca Empire's achievements in sustainable development continue to inspire modern efforts to create environmentally conscious and socially equitable societies.

7.4 SOCIETAL SHIFTS IN ATTITUDES TOWARD GROWTH AND CONTENTMENT

Historical shifts in societal attitudes toward growth and contentment often reflect broader changes in values, political structures, and economic conditions. These shifts reveal how societies redefine success and fulfillment in response to changing circumstances.

The Renaissance: A Reawakening of Growth and Creativity

The Renaissance, which began in the 14th century in Italy and spread across Europe, marked a period of profound cultural and intellectual growth. It was characterized by a renewed interest in the arts, sciences, and human potential. Renaissance thinkers and artists, such as Leonardo da Vinci and Michelangelo, pushed the boundaries of knowledge and creativity, reflecting a collective aspiration for growth and self-expression.

The Renaissance was also a period of social and economic transformation. The rise of trade, exploration, and scientific discovery contributed to a sense of limitless possibility. However, this pursuit of growth was balanced by a deep appreciation for beauty, harmony, and the classical ideals of balance and proportion.

The Renaissance illustrates how societies can flourish when growth is guided by a commitment to creativity, knowledge, and cultural enrichment.

The Industrial Revolution: Growth at the Expense of Contentment

The Industrial Revolution, which began in the 18th century, transformed societies through rapid industrialization, technological innovation, and economic expansion. While it led to unprecedented levels of productivity and material wealth, it also brought about significant social and environmental challenges.

Factory work replaced traditional crafts, leading to harsh working conditions, long hours, and social dislocation. The emphasis on economic growth often came at the expense of workers' well-being and environmental health, creating a disconnect between growth and contentment.

The Industrial Revolution serves as a cautionary tale of how the pursuit of growth, when not aligned with human and environmental well-being, can lead to widespread dissatisfaction and social upheaval.

7.5 CONCLUSION: HISTORICAL LESSONS FOR NAVIGATING CONTENTMENT AND GROWTH

Historical examples of individuals and societies illustrate the diverse ways in which contentment and growth have been pursued, defined, and understood. From the Buddha's spiritual journey to the rise and fall of empires, these stories provide valuable lessons on the importance of balance, sustainability, and ethical conduct.

By learning from history, we can better navigate our own paths to contentment and growth, drawing on the wisdom of those who came before us. As we move forward, let us consider how these historical lessons can inform our choices and guide us in creating a balanced and fulfilling life. Whether we are striving for personal achievements or contributing to the growth of our communities, the experiences of past individuals and societies remind us of the importance of cultivating inner peace, ethical values, and social harmony.

As we delve deeper into the exploration of contentment and growth, the historical perspective provides a grounding context that highlights the timeless nature of this paradox. These stories show that the tension between striving for more and being content with what we have is not a modern dilemma—it is a fundamental aspect of the human experience, one that has shaped the course of history and continues to influence our lives today.

CHAPTER 08

TECHNOLOGICAL IMPACT—HOW TECHNOLOGY SHAPES OUR PERCEPTION OF CONTENTMENT AND GROWTH

8.1 INTRODUCTION: THE TRANSFORMATIVE POWER OF TECHNOLOGY

Technology has fundamentally transformed the way we live, work, and interact with the world. It has brought unprecedented advancements in communication, healthcare, education, and productivity, enabling people to achieve more than ever before. Yet, it has also introduced new challenges, including information overload, social isolation, and a constant drive for progress that can undermine contentment.

This chapter explores the impact of technology on our perceptions of contentment and growth. We'll examine how technology influences our desires, shapes our expectations, and affects our ability to experience satisfaction. By understanding these dynamics, we can better navigate the complexities of living in a technologically driven world.

8.2 THE DOUBLE-EDGED SWORD: TECHNOLOGY AS A CATALYST FOR BOTH GROWTH AND DISSATISFACTION

Technology acts as a double-edged sword when it comes to growth and contentment. On one hand, it facilitates growth by expanding access to information, improving productivity, and creating new opportunities for learning and innovation. On the other hand, it can foster dissatisfaction by creating unrealistic expectations, amplifying social comparison, and perpetuating a sense of inadequacy.

The Role of Technology in Accelerating Personal and Societal Growth

Technology has been a driving force behind many of the most significant advances in human history. It has accelerated personal growth by providing access to educational resources, online courses, and virtual mentors. People can now learn new skills, connect with experts, and participate in global communities from anywhere in the world.

On a societal level, technological advancements have led to improved healthcare, increased life expectancy, and greater economic prosperity. Innovations such as renewable energy technologies, artificial intelligence, and biotechnology hold the promise of solving some of humanity's most pressing challenges.

Technology's capacity to enable growth is undeniable, but its impact on contentment is more complex. The same tools that facilitate growth can also create new sources of stress and dissatisfaction.

The Paradox of Choice: How Technology Creates Dissatisfaction

One of the paradoxical effects of technology is the phenomenon known as the *paradox of choice*. In his book *The Paradox of Choice: Why More Is Less*, psychologist Barry Schwartz argues that while having more choices can increase freedom, it can also lead to greater dissatisfaction. When people are faced with an overwhelming number of options—whether it be consumer products, career paths, or social activities—they often experience decision fatigue and regret.

Technology amplifies this paradox by presenting a seemingly infinite array of options. Online shopping platforms, social media, and digital content providers offer countless choices, making it difficult for people to feel satisfied with their decisions. This can lead to a perpetual search for better options, undermining the ability to experience contentment with what one already has.

Examples of the Paradox of Choice in the Digital Age

- **Streaming Services:** The abundance of streaming options can make it difficult for people to choose what to watch, leading to indecision and dissatisfaction.
- **Online Shopping:** E-commerce platforms provide access to a vast array of products, but the endless comparisons and reviews can result in decision paralysis and buyer's remorse.
- **Social Media:** The constant exposure to others' curated lives can create a sense of missing out or not measuring up, leading to dissatisfaction and envy.

By understanding the paradox of choice, individuals can make more intentional decisions and focus on what truly matters, reducing the negative impact of technology on contentment.

8.3 THE ROLE OF SOCIAL MEDIA: CONNECTING AND COMPETING

Social media has revolutionized how people connect, communicate, and share information. Platforms such as Facebook, Instagram, Twitter, and LinkedIn have become integral parts of modern life, enabling people to maintain relationships, network professionally, and stay informed. However, social media also has a darker side, contributing to social comparison, self-esteem issues, and a distorted perception of reality.

Social Media and the Amplification of Social Comparison

Social media platforms are designed to encourage users to share their accomplishments, experiences, and lifestyles. While this can foster connection and celebration, it can also lead to unhealthy social comparison. People often compare themselves to the idealized images of others, leading to feelings of inadequacy and discontent.

Research has shown that people who spend more time on social media are more likely to experience anxiety, depression, and lower self-esteem. This is partly because social media often presents a highlight reel of others' lives, creating a skewed perception that everyone else is happier, more successful, and more fulfilled.

The Impact of Social Media on Contentment

- **Envy and FOMO (Fear of Missing Out)**: Seeing others' achievements, vacations, or social gatherings can create envy and the fear of missing out, making people feel less satisfied with their own lives.
- **Pressure to Present a Perfect Image**: The pressure to present oneself in the best possible light can lead to anxiety and a sense of inauthenticity.
- **Distorted Reality**: Social media can distort reality by presenting an unrealistic standard of beauty, success, and happiness, making it difficult for people to appreciate their own lives.

Strategies for Managing the Impact of Social Media

To mitigate the negative effects of social media on contentment, individuals can adopt strategies such as:

- **Limiting Time on Social Media**: Reducing time spent on social media can decrease exposure to negative comparisons and increase time for more fulfilling activities.
- **Curating a Positive Feed**: Following accounts that promote positivity, authenticity, and well-being can create a more supportive social media environment.
- **Practicing Digital Detox**: Taking regular breaks from social media can help people reconnect with the present-moment and appreciate real-life experiences.

By using social media mindfully, individuals can harness its benefits while minimizing its impact on their sense of contentment and well-being.

8.4 TECHNOLOGY AND THE WORKPLACE: PRODUCTIVITY VS. WELL-BEING

The impact of technology on the workplace has been profound, changing how people work, communicate, and achieve professional growth. Digital tools and platforms have increased productivity and enabled remote work, but they have also blurred the boundaries between work and personal life, contributing to stress and burnout.

The Rise of Remote Work and Its Impact on Contentment

The COVID-19 pandemic accelerated the adoption of remote work, leading to a paradigm shift in how organizations operate. While remote work offers flexibility and reduces commuting time, it also presents new challenges, such as social isolation, work-life imbalance, and the pressure to be constantly available.

Challenges of Remote Work

- **Lack of Social Interaction**: Remote work can lead to feelings of loneliness and disconnection from colleagues, affecting job satisfaction and overall well-being.
- **Work-Life Imbalance**: The blurring of boundaries between work and personal life can result in longer working hours and increased stress.
- **Digital Fatigue**: The constant use of digital communication tools can lead to digital fatigue, reducing productivity and increasing burnout.

Organizations and employees must find ways to balance the benefits of remote work with strategies that promote well-being and contentment.

The Role of Technology in Workplace Growth and Innovation

Despite its challenges, technology has also created opportunities for growth and innovation in the workplace. Digital tools enable collaboration across geographies, access to global talent, and the development of new business models. Employees can leverage technology to learn new skills, advance their careers, and contribute to organizational success.

Organizations can foster growth and contentment in the workplace by adopting policies that prioritize employee well-being, including flexible work options, mental health support, and professional development opportunities.

8.5 THE FUTURE OF TECHNOLOGY AND HUMAN FULFILLMENT

As technology continues to evolve, its impact on contentment and growth will become even more complex. Emerging technologies such as artificial intelligence (AI), virtual reality (VR), and biotechnology hold the potential to revolutionize human experiences, but they also raise ethical and existential questions.

Artificial Intelligence and the Quest for Growth

AI has the potential to transform industries, solve complex problems, and enhance human capabilities. However, it also poses challenges related to job displacement, privacy, and decision-making. As AI systems become more integrated into daily life, individuals and societies must consider how to balance technological advancement with human well-being and ethical considerations.

Virtual Reality and the Experience of Contentment

VR technology offers immersive experiences that can enhance learning, entertainment, and social interaction. However, excessive use of VR could lead to a preference for virtual experiences over real-world engagement, potentially undermining contentment with reality.

Biotechnology and the Enhancement of Human Potential

Biotechnology, including genetic engineering and biohacking, has the potential to enhance physical and cognitive abilities, extend lifespan, and prevent diseases. While these advancements could promote growth and well-being, they also raise ethical concerns about equity, access, and the definition of what it means to be human.

The future of technology will require thoughtful consideration of how these innovations impact human fulfillment and the pursuit of a balanced life.

8.6 CONCLUSION: NAVIGATING THE TECHNOLOGICAL LANDSCAPE

Technology has transformed our understanding of contentment and growth, creating new opportunities and challenges. While it enables unprecedented levels of personal and societal growth, it can also foster dissatisfaction, amplify social comparison, and disrupt well-being.

By using technology mindfully, setting boundaries, and focusing on meaningful experiences, individuals can navigate the complexities of the technological landscape and create a balanced life that integrates growth and contentment.

As we continue our exploration, the role of technology serves as a reminder that growth and contentment are not just personal pursuits – they are shaped by the tools we use and the environments we create. Understanding these dynamics is key to achieving a harmonious relationship between technological progress and human fulfillment.

CHAPTER

ENVIRONMENTAL CONSIDERATIONS—BALANCING GROWTH AND SUSTAINABILITY

09

9.1 INTRODUCTION: THE ENVIRONMENTAL DIMENSION OF CONTENTMENT AND GROWTH

The relationship between growth and the environment has become one of the most critical issues of our time. As human activity continues to shape the natural world, the pursuit of growth often comes into conflict with the need for environmental preservation and sustainability. Striking a balance between economic development and ecological stability is essential for achieving long-term contentment, both for individuals and societies.

This chapter explores the environmental considerations of contentment and growth, examining how growth impacts the environment, the concept of sustainable development, and the role of environmental stewardship in promoting a balanced and fulfilling life. By understanding these dynamics, we can envision a future where growth and environmental health coexist in harmony.

9.2 THE IMPACT OF GROWTH ON THE ENVIRONMENT: CHALLENGES AND CONSEQUENCES

Economic growth and technological advancement have brought about remarkable improvements in human well-being, including higher life expectancy, better healthcare, and greater access to resources. However, these achievements have often come at a significant cost to the environment. The extraction of natural resources, industrial production, and the generation of waste and pollution have all contributed to environmental degradation and climate change.

Environmental Consequences of Unchecked Growth

1. **Resource Depletion**: The extraction of non-renewable resources, such as fossil fuels, minerals, and freshwater, has led to the depletion of critical natural reserves. This can create resource scarcity and undermine the capacity for future growth.
2. **Habitat Destruction and Biodiversity Loss**: Expanding agricultural, industrial, and urban areas has led to the destruction of habitats and the loss of biodiversity. Species extinction rates have accelerated, threatening the balance of ecosystems and the services they provide.
3. **Pollution and Climate Change**: The emission of greenhouse gases from industrial activities, transportation, and deforestation has contributed to global warming and climate change. Air, water, and soil pollution from industrial waste and chemical runoff have also impacted public health and the environment.
4. **Deforestation and Land Degradation**: The clearing of forests for agriculture and development has resulted in soil erosion, reduced carbon sequestration, and disrupted water cycles, further exacerbating climate change and environmental degradation.

These consequences highlight the need for a more sustainable approach to growth that considers the long-term health of the planet and the well-being of future generations.

The Tragedy of the Commons: A Model for Understanding Environmental Degradation

The concept of the *tragedy of the commons*, introduced by ecologist Garrett Hardin, illustrates how individual pursuit of growth can lead to collective environmental harm. When individuals or groups exploit shared resources, such as forests, fisheries, or the atmosphere, for their own benefit, they may deplete or degrade these resources, resulting in negative consequences for everyone.

The tragedy of the commons underscores the importance of collective action and regulation to ensure that growth does not come at the expense of shared environmental resources. It suggests that achieving a balance between growth and contentment requires a shift from individualistic behavior to a more community-oriented approach that prioritizes long-term sustainability.

9.3 SUSTAINABLE DEVELOPMENT: A FRAMEWORK FOR HARMONIZING GROWTH AND ENVIRONMENTAL HEALTH

Sustainable development offers a framework for achieving economic growth while preserving environmental health and promoting social equity. The concept of sustainable development was popularized by the 1987 Brundtland Report, which defined it as "development that meets the needs of the present without compromising the ability of future generations to meet their own needs."

The Three Pillars of Sustainable Development

1. **Economic Sustainability**: Economic sustainability involves creating growth that is financially viable in the long-term without depleting resources or causing environmental harm. It includes promoting efficient use of resources, supporting green technologies, and ensuring that economic activities contribute to social well-being.
2. **Social Sustainability**: Social sustainability focuses on creating inclusive and equitable societies where all people have access to basic needs, such as healthcare, education, and employment. It emphasizes the importance of social cohesion, cultural preservation, and community resilience.
3. **Environmental Sustainability**: Environmental sustainability aims to protect and restore natural ecosystems, reduce pollution and waste, and promote the sustainable use of natural resources. It involves minimizing human impact on the environment and ensuring that ecosystems can continue to provide essential services.

Achieving sustainable development requires integrating these three pillars and considering the long-term impacts of growth on both people and the planet.

Examples of Sustainable Development Initiatives

Many countries and organizations have implemented sustainable development initiatives to balance growth with environmental health. These initiatives include:

- **Renewable Energy Projects**: Investing in solar, wind, and hydropower technologies to reduce dependence on fossil fuels and decrease greenhouse gas emissions.
- **Sustainable Agriculture**: Implementing practices such as crop rotation, organic farming, and agroforestry to maintain soil health and biodiversity while producing food sustainably.
- **Circular Economy Models**: Designing products and systems that minimize waste and promote recycling, reuse, and resource efficiency.

These initiatives demonstrate that growth can be achieved while preserving the environment, provided sustainability is prioritized in policy and practice.

9.4 ENVIRONMENTAL CONTENTMENT: FINDING FULFILLMENT IN SUSTAINABILITY

Environmental contentment involves finding fulfillment and satisfaction through practices that promote environmental stewardship and sustainability. This approach shifts the focus from acquiring more material possessions to appreciating the natural world and living in harmony with the environment.

The Philosophy of Voluntary Simplicity

The philosophy of voluntary simplicity advocates for a lifestyle that is less focused on material consumption and more oriented toward meaningful experiences, environmental stewardship, and personal well-being. People who practice voluntary simplicity often prioritize:

- **Minimalism**: Reducing unnecessary possessions and focusing on quality over quantity.
- **Mindful Consumption**: Making conscious choices about what to buy and how to use resources, with an emphasis on sustainability and ethical production.

- **Connection with Nature**: Spending time in nature, gardening, or engaging in outdoor activities to foster a deeper appreciation for the environment.

By embracing voluntary simplicity, individuals can experience a sense of contentment that is not tied to material growth but is rooted in environmental awareness and personal fulfillment.

Environmental Activism and Advocacy

Environmental activism and advocacy offer pathways to achieving contentment by contributing to positive change. Many people find fulfillment in working to protect the environment, whether through grassroots activism, conservation efforts, or policy advocacy.

Examples of Environmental Advocacy

- Participating in reforestation projects or community clean-up events.
- Supporting policies that promote renewable energy, biodiversity conservation, and climate action.
- Engaging in education and awareness campaigns to promote sustainable practices.

Environmental activism provides a sense of purpose and connection to a larger cause, fostering a form of contentment that arises from contributing to the well-being of the planet.

9.5 THE ROLE OF TECHNOLOGY IN PROMOTING ENVIRONMENTAL CONTENTMENT AND GROWTH

Technology can play a pivotal role in supporting both growth and environmental contentment. Innovations such as green technologies, smart cities, and digital platforms for environmental monitoring offer new ways to promote sustainability while enhancing quality of life.

Green Technologies and Sustainable Innovation

Green technologies, such as electric vehicles, energy-efficient buildings, and carbon capture systems, contribute to environmental sustainability by reducing pollution and resource consumption. These technologies enable societies to continue growing economically while minimizing environmental impact.

Examples of Green Technology Innovations

- **Electric Vehicles (EVs)**: EVs reduce greenhouse gas emissions and dependence on fossil fuels, promoting cleaner air and lower carbon footprints.
- **Smart Agriculture**: Technologies such as precision farming, which uses sensors and data analytics to optimize crop production, can increase yields while reducing water and fertilizer use.
- **Sustainable Architecture**: Green buildings incorporate energy-efficient designs, renewable energy sources, and sustainable materials, reducing their environmental impact.

By investing in green technologies, societies can create pathways for sustainable growth that align with environmental preservation.

The Role of Digital Platforms and Data in Environmental Management

Digital platforms and data analytics play an increasingly important role in environmental management. Remote sensing, satellite imaging, and data visualization tools enable governments, organizations, and communities to monitor environmental changes, track pollution levels, and develop targeted interventions.

Examples of Digital Platforms for Environmental Monitoring

- **Global Forest Watch**: An online platform that uses satellite data to monitor deforestation in real time.
- **Climate Prediction Tools**: Models that simulate future climate scenarios based on current emissions and environmental policies.

- **Citizen Science Apps**: Apps that enable individuals to report environmental observations, such as bird sightings or water quality, contributing to collective data and research.

Digital technologies empower individuals and communities to engage with environmental issues and contribute to sustainable solutions, enhancing both growth and contentment.

9.6 CONCLUSION: CREATING A SUSTAINABLE FUTURE OF CONTENTMENT AND GROWTH

The relationship between contentment and growth is deeply intertwined with the health of the environment. As we face growing environmental challenges, it is essential to rethink how we pursue growth and define contentment. Sustainable development offers a pathway to achieving economic prosperity without sacrificing ecological balance.

By adopting sustainable practices, embracing environmental stewardship, and using technology for good, we can achieve growth that harmonizes with environmental well-being, benefiting both current and future generations.

As we continue to explore the complexities of contentment and growth, the environmental perspective serves as a reminder that our well-being is inextricably linked to the well-being of the planet. Achieving balance between these forces is not just a personal or societal challenge—it is a global imperative that will shape the future of humanity.

CHAPTER

PERSONAL DEVELOPMENT—STRATEGIES FOR BALANCING CONTENTMENT AND GROWTH

10

10.1 INTRODUCTION: THE PERSONAL DIMENSION OF CONTENTMENT AND GROWTH

The pursuit of contentment and growth is not only a societal and philosophical issue—it is also deeply personal. Each individual's journey involves navigating the tension between striving for more and appreciating what one has. Personal development practices can help people find this balance, fostering a sense of fulfillment while promoting continuous growth.

This chapter explores strategies for personal development that support both contentment and growth. We'll discuss approaches such as cultivating a growth mindset, practicing mindfulness and self-compassion, setting meaningful goals, and developing habits that support well-being. By integrating these practices into daily life, individuals can create a harmonious relationship between their desire for progress and their capacity for satisfaction.

10.2 CULTIVATING A GROWTH MINDSET: EMBRACING CHALLENGES AND LEARNING

The concept of a *growth mindset*, introduced by psychologist Carol Dweck, describes the belief that abilities and intelligence can be developed through effort, learning, and perseverance. In contrast, a *fixed mindset* involves the belief that abilities are innate and unchangeable. Cultivating a growth mindset is essential for achieving personal growth and maintaining a sense of contentment amid challenges.

Characteristics of a Growth Mindset

People with a growth mindset view challenges as opportunities for learning, see failures as stepping stones to success, and embrace effort as a necessary part of improvement. This mindset fosters resilience and adaptability, enabling individuals to pursue growth without becoming discouraged by setbacks.

Key Traits of a Growth Mindset

- **Embracing Challenges**: Viewing obstacles as opportunities to learn and grow.
- **Persistence**: Continuing to strive despite difficulties and setbacks.
- **Effort**: Recognizing that effort is essential for developing new skills and achieving mastery.
- **Learning from Criticism**: Using feedback as a tool for improvement rather than a judgment of one's abilities.
- **Finding Inspiration in Others**: Viewing others' success as a source of motivation and learning rather than a threat.

Strategies for Developing a Growth Mindset

1. **Reframe Negative Self-Talk**: Replace thoughts like "I'm not good at this" with "I'm still learning, and I can improve with practice."
2. **Set Learning Goals Instead of Performance Goals**: Focus on what you can learn from an experience rather than on achieving a specific outcome.
3. **Embrace the Process**: Appreciate the journey of learning and self-improvement rather than fixating on the end result.
4. **Celebrate Small Wins**: Acknowledge progress and small achievements along the way to reinforce the belief in your ability to grow.

Cultivating a growth mindset helps individuals approach life with curiosity, resilience, and a sense of purpose, contributing to both personal growth and lasting contentment.

10.3 PRACTICING MINDFULNESS AND SELF-COMPASSION: FINDING CONTENTMENT IN THE PRESENT-MOMENT

Mindfulness is the practice of paying attention to the present-moment with non-judgmental awareness. It involves observing thoughts, emotions, and sensations as they arise without becoming attached or reacting impulsively. Mindfulness helps individuals find contentment in the present-moment, reducing the tendency to constantly seek more or dwell on the past.

The Benefits of Mindfulness for Contentment and Growth

Research has shown that mindfulness practices can reduce stress, increase emotional regulation, and improve overall well-being. By fostering a state of present-moment awareness, mindfulness helps individuals appreciate their current experiences and cultivate a sense of inner peace.

Benefits of Mindfulness

- **Reduced Anxiety and Stress**: Mindfulness decreases the mental clutter that contributes to anxiety and stress.
- **Enhanced Self-Awareness**: Mindfulness promotes a deeper understanding of one's thoughts, emotions, and behaviors.
- **Improved Focus and Concentration**: Mindfulness strengthens the ability to focus on tasks and remain present.
- **Greater Emotional Resilience**: Mindfulness helps individuals respond to difficult emotions with calmness and clarity.

Integrating Mindfulness into Daily Life

Mindfulness can be practiced in various ways, from formal meditation to simple daily activities. Techniques for integrating mindfulness include:

1. **Mindful Breathing**: Focus on the breath as it flows in and out. Observe the sensations of breathing without trying to change it.
2. **Body Scan Meditation**: Bring awareness to different parts of the body, noticing any sensations, tension, or relaxation.

3. **Mindful Eating**: Eat slowly and attentively, savoring each bite and observing the taste, texture, and aroma of the food.
4. **Mindful Walking**: Walk slowly and pay attention to each step, the feeling of the ground beneath your feet, and the sights and sounds around you.
5. **Gratitude Practice**: Reflect on the things you are grateful for, cultivating a sense of appreciation for the present-moment.

By incorporating mindfulness into daily routines, individuals can cultivate a state of contentment that is independent of external circumstances.

The Role of Self-Compassion

Self-compassion, as defined by psychologist Kristin Neff, involves treating oneself with kindness and understanding during times of difficulty or perceived failure. It means acknowledging one's suffering and imperfections without harsh self-criticism or judgment.

Elements of Self-Compassion

- **Self-Kindness**: Being gentle and supportive toward oneself rather than harsh or critical.
- **Common Humanity**: Recognizing that suffering and failure are part of the shared human experience.
- **Mindfulness**: Observing one's thoughts and emotions with openness and acceptance.

Practicing self-compassion fosters emotional resilience, reduces self-doubt, and promotes a healthy balance between striving for growth and accepting oneself as one is.

10.4 SETTING MEANINGFUL GOALS: ALIGNING ASPIRATIONS WITH VALUES

Goal-setting is a powerful tool for personal growth, but not all goals contribute to lasting contentment. Meaningful goals are those that align with one's values, passions, and purpose, providing a sense of direction and fulfillment.

The Characteristics of Meaningful Goals

Meaningful goals have several key characteristics:

- **Intrinsic Motivation**: They are driven by internal desires, such as personal growth or contribution, rather than external rewards or pressures.
- **Alignment with Values**: They reflect what is truly important to the individual and are connected to a sense of purpose.
- **Growth-Oriented**: They challenge individuals to expand their abilities, knowledge, or perspectives.
- **Realistic and Attainable**: While they may be challenging, meaningful goals are also achievable and realistic.

The Process of Setting and Achieving Meaningful Goals

1. **Clarify Your Values**: Reflect on what is most important to you. What values guide your decisions and actions? Examples of values include creativity, compassion, integrity, and learning.
2. **Identify Long-Term Aspirations**: Think about where you want to be in five, ten, or twenty years. What legacy do you want to leave? What would make your life meaningful?
3. **Set Short-Term and Mid-Term Goals**: Break long-term aspirations into smaller, actionable goals that can be achieved in the short or mid-term.
4. **Create a Plan of Action**: Develop a step-by-step plan to achieve each goal. Include specific actions, timelines, and potential challenges.
5. **Monitor and Adjust**: Regularly review your goals and adjust them as needed based on your experiences and changing circumstances.

By setting meaningful goals, individuals can pursue growth in a way that contributes to lasting fulfillment and aligns with their authentic selves.

10.5 DEVELOPING HABITS THAT SUPPORT CONTENTMENT AND GROWTH

Habits play a crucial role in shaping personal development and well-being. Positive habits support growth and contentment by reinforcing healthy behaviors, fostering resilience, and creating a sense of stability.

The Power of Small Habits

Small habits, repeated consistently over time, can lead to significant changes. James Clear, author of *Atomic Habits*, emphasizes that small habits are the building blocks of long-term success. Focusing on tiny, incremental changes helps individuals avoid overwhelm and build momentum.

Examples of Small Habits for Personal Growth

- **Reading for 10 Minutes Daily**: Expanding knowledge and stimulating personal growth.
- **Journaling Each Morning**: Reflecting on thoughts and emotions, setting intentions for the day.
- **Exercising for 15 Minutes**: Improving physical health and mental clarity.
- **Practicing Gratitude**: Writing down three things you are grateful for each day.

Creating Positive Habit Loops

Positive habits are reinforced by creating habit loops that include a cue, a routine, and a reward. For example, if the goal is to develop a habit of exercising in the morning, the cue might be setting out workout clothes the night before, the routine would be performing the exercise, and the reward could be a sense of accomplishment and a healthy breakfast.

By creating positive habit loops, individuals can establish routines that promote both personal growth and contentment.

10.6 CONCLUSION: THE PERSONAL PATH TO BALANCED GROWTH AND CONTENTMENT

Personal development is a lifelong journey that involves balancing the desire for growth with the experience of contentment. By cultivating a growth mindset, practicing mindfulness and self-compassion, setting meaningful goals, and developing positive habits, individuals can create a fulfilling and balanced life.

The strategies discussed in this chapter provide tools for navigating the complexities of personal growth and satisfaction. By integrating these practices into daily life, individuals can achieve a sense of harmony between striving for more and appreciating what they have, fostering a life of both achievement and inner peace.

CHAPTER

CREATIVITY AND INNOVATION—THE RELATIONSHIP BETWEEN CONTENTMENT AND CREATIVE OUTPUT

11

11.1 INTRODUCTION: CREATIVITY AS A PATHWAY TO GROWTH AND FULFILLMENT

Creativity and innovation are often associated with personal growth, self-expression, and societal advancement. Whether through art, science, business, or technology, creative endeavors drive progress and bring about new ideas, solutions, and experiences. Yet, the creative process also involves moments of stillness, reflection, and contentment. Understanding the relationship between contentment and creativity can provide insights into how these two forces interact and contribute to a fulfilling life.

This chapter explores how contentment influences creativity and how periods of growth and stagnation can inspire innovation. By examining the role of contentment in the creative process, we can gain a deeper understanding of how to foster creativity while maintaining a sense of satisfaction and balance.

11.2 THE CREATIVE PROCESS: BALANCING INSPIRATION AND EXECUTION

Creativity is not a linear process but a dynamic interplay between inspiration, exploration, and execution. It involves periods of active engagement as well as moments of rest and reflection. The creative process often requires stepping back, allowing ideas to simmer, and finding contentment in the journey rather than focusing solely on the outcome.

The Role of Contentment in Fostering Creativity

Contentment can serve as a fertile ground for creativity. When individuals are at peace with themselves and their circumstances, they are more likely to explore new ideas and take creative risks without fear of failure. Contentment creates a sense of psychological safety that allows people to think freely, experiment, and push boundaries.

How Contentment Enhances Creativity

- **Reduces Performance Pressure**: When people are content, they are less driven by external validation and more focused on intrinsic motivation, allowing them to pursue creativity for its own sake.
- **Promotes Divergent Thinking**: Contentment fosters a relaxed state of mind, which is conducive to divergent thinking—the ability to generate multiple, diverse ideas and perspectives.
- **Encourages Playfulness and Exploration**: Contentment enables individuals to approach creative activities with a sense of playfulness and curiosity, which are essential for innovation.

However, excessive contentment can sometimes lead to complacency, reducing the drive to create or solve problems. The key is to find a balance between contentment and the desire to grow and explore new possibilities.

The Tension Between Contentment and Creative Ambition

While contentment can support creativity, many creative individuals are also driven by a sense of dissatisfaction or restlessness. This tension between contentment and creative ambition can serve as a powerful motivator, pushing individuals to seek new forms of expression or to challenge existing norms.

Examples of Creative Tension

- Many great works of art, literature, and music have been born out of periods of personal struggle, introspection, or dissatisfaction.
- Scientists and innovators often pursue breakthroughs out of a desire to solve pressing problems or address gaps in knowledge, reflecting a form of creative dissatisfaction.

Understanding this dynamic tension helps explain why some of the most profound creative achievements emerge from a place of both contentment and longing for more.

11.3 CREATIVITY AND FLOW: ACHIEVING OPTIMAL EXPERIENCE AND FULFILLMENT

The concept of *flow*, introduced by psychologist Mihaly Csikszentmihalyi, describes a state of complete immersion and engagement in an activity. Flow is often referred to as being 'in the zone', where the challenges of the task match one's skills, leading to a sense of effortless involvement and deep satisfaction.

The Characteristics of Flow in Creative Work

Flow is characterized by several key elements that are particularly relevant to creative endeavors:

1. **Clear Goals and Immediate Feedback**: People in a flow state have clear objectives and receive immediate feedback on their progress, which keeps them engaged and motivated.
2. **Balance Between Challenge and Skill**: Flow occurs when the difficulty of the task is slightly above one's skill level, creating a sense of mastery and enjoyment.
3. **Loss of Self-Consciousness**: In a flow state, people become so absorbed in the activity that they lose awareness of themselves and their surroundings, experiencing a sense of timelessness and focus.
4. **Intrinsic Motivation**: Flow is driven by intrinsic motivation, meaning that the activity is pursued for its own sake rather than for external rewards or recognition.

Fostering Flow to Enhance Creativity and Growth

Creating the conditions for flow can enhance both creativity and personal growth. Strategies for fostering flow include:

- **Setting Clear and Challenging Goals**: Choose creative projects that push your abilities without overwhelming you.
- **Eliminating Distractions**: Create a focused environment that minimizes interruptions and allows deep concentration.
- **Embracing Feedback and Iteration**: Seek feedback on your creative work and use it to refine and improve your ideas.
- **Engaging in Regular Practice**: Consistent practice helps build the skills necessary to enter a flow state more easily.

Flow provides a pathway to achieving growth and contentment simultaneously, as individuals experience deep fulfillment through their creative engagement.

11.4 THE IMPACT OF DISCONTENT ON CREATIVE OUTPUT

While contentment can foster creativity, discontent and dissatisfaction can also serve as powerful catalysts for creative expression. Feelings of frustration, longing, or restlessness often drive individuals to explore new ideas, challenge the status quo, and seek innovative solutions.

Creative Discontent as a Source of Innovation

Many groundbreaking inventions and works of art have been born out of a desire to address personal or societal challenges. For example:

- **Vincent van Gogh**: Despite experiencing intense personal turmoil, van Gogh created some of the most vibrant and expressive artworks in history. His paintings reflect both his inner struggles and his quest for beauty and meaning.
- **Steve Jobs**: As a visionary entrepreneur, Steve Jobs often expressed dissatisfaction with existing technology, which drove him to innovate and create products that transformed the way people interact with technology.

Creative discontent is not necessarily negative – it can inspire people to question assumptions, explore new possibilities, and pursue change. However, it is important to manage discontent constructively to avoid burnout or destructive behavior.

Finding Balance Between Discontent and Contentment

Balancing discontent with contentment involves acknowledging the value of both states. While discontent can inspire growth and innovation, contentment provides the emotional stability and well-being needed to sustain creative efforts over the long-term. Practices such as mindfulness, self-reflection, and gratitude can help individuals find equilibrium between these two forces.

11.5 CREATIVITY AS A FORM OF PERSONAL GROWTH AND SELF-ACTUALIZATION

Creativity is not just about producing new ideas or products—it is also a form of personal growth and self-actualization. Through creative activities, individuals explore their inner worlds, express their values and emotions, and connect with others on a deeper level.

Creativity and Self-Expression

Creative expression allows individuals to communicate their thoughts, feelings, and identities in ways that words alone cannot capture. Whether through painting, writing, music, or dance, creative activities provide an outlet for exploring and sharing one's inner experiences.

Benefits of Creative Self-Expression

- **Emotional Release**: Creativity offers a healthy way to process and release emotions, reducing stress and enhancing emotional well-being.
- **Identity Exploration**: Creative work enables individuals to explore different aspects of their identity, beliefs, and values.
- **Connection with Others**: Creative expression can foster a sense of connection and empathy, as others resonate with shared themes and experiences.

Creativity and Meaning-Making

Creativity is also a way of making sense of the world and finding meaning in one's experiences. People use creative activities to reflect on personal challenges, celebrate achievements, and explore existential questions. This process of meaning-making contributes to a sense of fulfillment and personal growth.

11.6 ENCOURAGING CREATIVITY IN DAILY LIFE: PRACTICES FOR FOSTERING INNOVATION AND FULFILLMENT

Encouraging creativity in daily life involves cultivating habits and mindsets that support imaginative thinking, exploration, and expression. Strategies for fostering creativity include:

1. **Creating a Creative Routine**: Establish a regular time and space for creative activities, whether it's writing, drawing, or brainstorming.
2. **Engaging in Cross-Disciplinary Learning**: Explore subjects outside your usual areas of interest to gain new perspectives and ideas.
3. **Embracing Playfulness**: Approach creative activities with a sense of play and curiosity, rather than focusing solely on results.
4. **Keeping a Creative Journal**: Use a journal to capture ideas, sketches, or reflections that can serve as inspiration for future projects.
5. **Collaborating with Others**: Engage in collaborative projects to combine different strengths, ideas, and viewpoints.

By integrating creativity into everyday life, individuals can experience the joy and fulfillment that come from expressing their unique perspectives and contributing to the world.

11.7 CONCLUSION: CREATIVITY AND THE DANCE BETWEEN CONTENTMENT AND GROWTH

Creativity is a dynamic interplay between contentment and growth, where moments of peace and stillness fuel inspiration, and the desire for innovation drives exploration. By understanding this relationship, individuals can harness both contentment and discontent to produce meaningful and impactful work.

The creative journey is not just about achieving specific outcomes but about embracing the process of self-expression, discovery, and growth. As we continue our exploration of contentment and growth, creativity serves as a reminder that these forces are not opposites but complementary aspects of a fulfilling and balanced life.

CHAPTER

ETHICS AND MORALITY—BALANCING INDIVIDUAL SATISFACTION AND SOCIETAL ADVANCEMENT

12

12.1 INTRODUCTION: THE ETHICAL DIMENSIONS OF CONTENTMENT AND GROWTH

The pursuit of contentment and growth is not merely a personal endeavor—it also has ethical and moral implications for society as a whole. How we define success, prioritize goals, and allocate resources can impact not only our own well-being but also the well-being of others. Ethical considerations arise when individual aspirations conflict with collective needs or when personal growth comes at the expense of others' contentment.

This chapter explores the ethical and moral dimensions of contentment and growth, examining questions such as: Is it ethical to prioritize personal satisfaction over societal advancement? What responsibilities do individuals have toward others in their pursuit of growth? How can we balance individual and collective well-being? By addressing these questions, we can develop a more nuanced understanding of how to pursue growth and contentment in an ethically responsible manner.

12.2 MORAL IMPLICATIONS OF PRIORITIZING CONTENTMENT OR GROWTH

The decision to prioritize either contentment or growth often involves ethical trade-offs. For example, striving for personal success might lead to increased wealth and status, but it could also contribute to social inequality or environmental harm. Similarly, choosing to focus solely on contentment may promote personal well-being but could limit one's contributions to societal progress.

Ethical Dilemmas in the Pursuit of Personal Growth

The pursuit of personal growth can sometimes create ethical dilemmas, especially when it conflicts with the interests or well-being of others. Consider the following scenarios:

- **Career Advancement vs. Family Time**: An individual may choose to prioritize career growth by working long hours and taking on additional responsibilities. While this may lead to professional success, it can also strain relationships with family members and reduce quality time spent with loved ones.
- **Wealth Accumulation vs. Social Responsibility**: A person who seeks financial growth might accumulate significant wealth but choose not to contribute to social causes or support those in need. This raises ethical questions about the use of resources and the responsibilities that come with privilege.
- **Innovation vs. Ethical Boundaries**: In the pursuit of technological or scientific innovation, individuals and organizations may push ethical boundaries, such as experimenting with new technologies that have potential risks for society or the environment.

These scenarios highlight the importance of considering the broader impact of personal growth on others and making ethical choices that align with values such as fairness, compassion, and social responsibility.

Ethical Considerations in Pursuing Contentment

Prioritizing contentment can also raise ethical questions, particularly when it involves withdrawing from societal engagement or avoiding responsibilities. For example:

- **Choosing Personal Peace Over Social Activism**: A person may choose to prioritize personal contentment by avoiding stressful or challenging situations, such as participating in social activism or confronting injustice. While this may protect individual well-being, it could also perpetuate societal problems by failing to address them.

- **Contentment Through Ignorance**: In some cases, people may achieve contentment by ignoring or minimizing the suffering of others. This raises ethical concerns about the morality of contentment that is achieved at the expense of awareness or empathy.

These examples suggest that contentment, like growth, should be pursued with an awareness of its impact on others and a commitment to ethical principles.

12.3 BALANCING INDIVIDUAL SATISFACTION AND SOCIETAL ADVANCEMENT

Finding a balance between individual satisfaction and societal advancement is a complex ethical challenge. While personal growth and contentment are important for individual well-being, they must be considered in the context of broader societal goals, such as social equity, environmental sustainability, and collective well-being.

The Role of Social Responsibility in Personal Growth

Social responsibility involves recognizing the interconnectedness of personal actions and societal outcomes. It means considering how individual pursuits of growth and contentment contribute to or detract from the well-being of others.

Ways to Practice Social Responsibility in Personal Growth

- **Supporting Social Causes**: Contributing time, resources, or skills to support social causes that promote equality, justice, and well-being.
- **Engaging in Ethical Consumerism**: Making purchasing decisions that align with values such as environmental sustainability, fair labor practices, and cruelty-free products.
- **Advocating for Positive Change**: Using one's voice, platform, or influence to advocate for policies or practices that benefit society as a whole.

By integrating social responsibility into personal growth, individuals can contribute to societal advancement while pursuing their own aspirations.

Collective Well-Being as a Measure of Success

In many cultures and philosophies, collective well-being is considered a measure of true success. This perspective emphasizes that individual growth should not come at the expense of others' contentment and that a successful society is one where all members have the opportunity to thrive.

For example, the concept of *Ubuntu*, a philosophy from Southern Africa, emphasizes the interconnectedness of all people and the idea that 'I am because we are'. This philosophy suggests that individual well-being is inherently linked to the well-being of the community and that true growth involves uplifting others as well as oneself.

Embracing collective well-being as a measure of success challenges the notion of growth as purely individualistic and promotes a more holistic and ethical approach to personal and societal advancement.

12.4 ETHICAL FRAMEWORKS FOR BALANCING CONTENTMENT AND GROWTH

Several ethical frameworks can guide individuals in balancing contentment and growth in a morally responsible manner. These frameworks provide tools for making ethical decisions that consider the impact of personal actions on others and align with broader values.

Utilitarianism: Maximizing Overall Happiness

Utilitarianism is an ethical framework that focuses on maximizing overall happiness or well-being. It suggests that actions should be evaluated based on their consequences and that the most ethical choice is the one that produces the greatest good for the greatest number.

Applying Utilitarianism to Contentment and Growth

- Evaluate personal decisions based on their potential impact on the well-being of others.
- Consider how the pursuit of growth or contentment contributes to or detracts from collective happiness.

- Seek to achieve personal growth and satisfaction in ways that also enhance the well-being of others.

Utilitarianism encourages individuals to think beyond their own interests and consider the broader implications of their choices.

Deontology: Adhering to Moral Duties and Principles

Deontology is an ethical framework that emphasizes the importance of adhering to moral duties and principles, regardless of the consequences. It suggests that certain actions are inherently right or wrong and should be followed based on ethical rules.

Applying Deontology to Contentment and Growth

- Identify core moral principles, such as honesty, integrity, and respect for others, and ensure that personal pursuits align with these values.
- Avoid actions that violate ethical principles, even if they seem to lead to personal or societal growth.
- Consider the moral duties that individuals have toward others, such as fairness, compassion, and justice.

Deontology provides a clear set of guidelines for making ethical decisions that prioritize principles over outcomes.

Virtue Ethics: Cultivating Character and Moral Virtues

Virtue ethics focuses on the cultivation of moral virtues, such as courage, humility, generosity, and wisdom. It suggests that ethical behavior arises from developing a virtuous character and making choices that reflect one's best self.

Applying Virtue Ethics to Contentment and Growth

- Reflect on the virtues that are important for personal and societal well-being and strive to embody these qualities in daily life.
- Make decisions that contribute to personal growth and contentment while also demonstrating virtues such as kindness, empathy, and fairness.

- Consider how personal actions align with the values and virtues that define a good and meaningful life.

Virtue ethics encourages individuals to pursue growth and contentment in ways that cultivate moral character and contribute to the greater good.

12.5 CREATING AN ETHICAL FRAMEWORK FOR PERSONAL GROWTH AND CONTENTMENT

Creating a personal ethical framework for growth and contentment involves defining one's values, identifying guiding principles, and considering the impact of personal decisions on others. This framework can serve as a guide for making ethical choices that support both personal well-being and societal advancement.

Steps to Create an Ethical Framework

1. **Identify Core Values**: Reflect on the values that are most important to you, such as integrity, compassion, creativity, or social justice.
2. **Define Ethical Principles**: Determine the ethical principles that will guide your actions, such as honesty, fairness, and respect for others.
3. **Consider the Impact on Others**: Evaluate how your pursuit of growth or contentment affects the well-being of others and whether it aligns with your values and principles.
4. **Make Ethical Choices**: Use your ethical framework to make decisions that balance personal satisfaction with social responsibility.
5. **Reflect and Adjust**: Regularly reflect on your choices and their outcomes. Adjust your framework as needed to ensure it continues to align with your evolving values and circumstances.

By developing and applying an ethical framework, individuals can pursue personal growth and contentment in a way that is both fulfilling and socially responsible.

12.6 CONCLUSION: BALANCING ETHICS AND PERSONAL FULFILLMENT

The pursuit of contentment and growth is deeply intertwined with ethical and moral considerations. By recognizing the impact of personal decisions on others and embracing ethical principles, individuals can create a balance that supports both personal fulfillment and societal advancement.

Ethical frameworks such as utilitarianism, deontology, and virtue ethics provide valuable tools for making responsible choices that align with core values and contribute to the greater good. As we continue to explore the complexities of contentment and growth, ethics and morality remind us that true fulfillment is not just about achieving personal goals—it is also about living in harmony with others and contributing to a just and compassionate world.

CHAPTER

FUTURE PROJECTIONS—SPECULATING ON THE FUTURE OF CONTENTMENT AND GROWTH

13

13.1 INTRODUCTION: THE FUTURE OF CONTENTMENT AND GROWTH IN A CHANGING WORLD

As we move further into the 21st century, the dynamics of contentment and growth are likely to evolve in response to technological advancements, environmental challenges, shifting societal values, and changing economic landscapes. The future of contentment and growth will be shaped by how individuals and societies navigate these transformations and adapt to new realities.

This chapter explores speculative scenarios and potential paradigm shifts that could redefine contentment and growth in the future. We'll consider how emerging trends and challenges, such as artificial intelligence, climate change, and the evolving nature of work, might impact our understanding of fulfillment and progress. By examining these possibilities, we can better prepare for a future that supports both personal well-being and collective advancement.

13.2 THE IMPACT OF TECHNOLOGICAL ADVANCEMENTS ON CONTENTMENT AND GROWTH

Technology has always played a central role in shaping human experiences of contentment and growth. As we enter an era of rapid technological change, new innovations will continue to transform how people pursue satisfaction and progress.

The Rise of Artificial Intelligence and Human Potential

Artificial intelligence (AI) is poised to revolutionize industries, education, healthcare, and daily life. AI systems have the potential to enhance human capabilities, automate routine tasks, and provide personalized recommendations for learning, wellness, and productivity. However, the integration of AI into society also raises questions about its impact on contentment and growth.

Potential Scenarios

- **Enhanced Learning and Personal Development**: AI could enable personalized education and skill development, helping individuals achieve growth in areas that align with their strengths and interests.
- **AI-Driven Mental Health Support**: AI-based tools could provide mental health support, helping individuals manage stress, anxiety, and other challenges that impact contentment.
- **Job Displacement and Economic Inequality**: The automation of jobs could lead to economic inequality and job displacement, potentially reducing contentment and increasing social tensions.

The challenge will be to harness AI in ways that promote human well-being and minimize negative consequences. Policies that ensure equitable access to AI benefits, support reskilling and upskilling, and address ethical concerns will be essential for balancing growth and contentment in an AI-driven world.

Virtual Reality and the Experience of Contentment

Virtual reality (VR) and augmented reality (AR) technologies are creating new ways for people to experience contentment and growth. These technologies can provide immersive experiences that enhance learning, entertainment, and social interaction.

Potential Scenarios

- **Virtual Travel and Exploration**: VR could enable individuals to explore virtual worlds, visit distant places, or experience historical events, enriching their lives and broadening their perspectives.

- **Virtual Therapy and Mindfulness**: VR could be used for therapeutic purposes, such as guided meditations, relaxation exercises, and exposure therapy, supporting mental health and contentment.
- **Escapism and Overreliance on Virtual Experiences**: There is a risk that people may become overly reliant on virtual experiences, potentially neglecting real-world connections and activities.

While VR offers exciting possibilities for enhancing contentment and growth, it will be important to use these technologies mindfully, ensuring that they complement rather than replace real-world experiences.

13.3 CLIMATE CHANGE AND THE LIMITS OF GROWTH

Climate change is one of the most pressing global challenges of our time. The effects of it, such as extreme weather events, rising sea levels, and biodiversity loss, are likely to disrupt traditional models of economic growth and challenge our understanding of contentment.

The Concept of 'Limits to Growth'

The idea of 'limits to growth' was popularized by the 1972 report *The Limits to Growth*, which warned that unchecked economic and population growth would lead to resource depletion and environmental collapse. As climate change accelerates, the concept of limits to growth is becoming increasingly relevant.

Potential Scenarios

- **Sustainable Growth Models**: Societies may adopt new growth models that prioritize environmental sustainability, resource efficiency, and well-being over material expansion.
- **Shifts in Values and Lifestyles**: In response to environmental challenges, people may place greater value on simplicity, conservation, and community rather than material wealth and consumption.
- **Climate-Induced Migration and Conflict**: Climate change could lead to displacement, migration, and conflict over resources, posing challenges for achieving both growth and contentment.

Addressing climate change will require rethinking traditional notions of growth and embracing sustainable practices that promote resilience, equity, and environmental stewardship.

13.4 THE EVOLVING NATURE OF WORK AND ITS IMPACT ON FULFILLMENT

The nature of work is changing rapidly due to technological advancements, globalization, and shifting societal expectations. The future of work will have significant implications for how people experience contentment and growth, particularly as traditional career paths and job structures are disrupted.

The Rise of the Gig Economy and Freelance Work

The gig economy, characterized by short-term contracts and freelance work, is becoming increasingly prevalent. While this model offers flexibility and autonomy, it can also lead to job insecurity, lack of benefits, and increased stress.

Potential Scenarios

- **Increased Autonomy and Flexibility**: Individuals may experience greater autonomy and flexibility in choosing when, where, and how they work, contributing to higher satisfaction and work-life balance.
- **Challenges of Job Security and Benefits**: The lack of stable employment and benefits could lead to financial insecurity, reducing contentment and increasing anxiety.
- **The Need for New Social Safety Nets**: As traditional job structures change, there will be a need for new social safety nets, such as universal basic income or portable benefits, to support workers in achieving contentment and growth.

Navigating the evolving nature of work will require rethinking policies and practices to ensure that people can achieve both professional growth and personal well-being.

The Role of Lifelong Learning and Reskilling

In a rapidly changing world, the ability to continuously learn and adapt will be essential for personal growth and contentment. Lifelong learning and reskilling initiatives can help individuals stay relevant in the job market and pursue fulfilling careers.

Potential Scenarios

- **Personalized Learning Paths**: AI and digital platforms could enable personalized learning paths that align with individuals' interests and career goals.
- **Learning as a Source of Fulfillment**: Lifelong learning can become a source of fulfillment, enabling people to explore new subjects, develop new skills, and engage in meaningful pursuits.
- **Bridging the Skills Gap**: Investing in education and training can help bridge the skills gap and create opportunities for economic growth and personal development.

By embracing lifelong learning and creating opportunities for growth, societies can support individuals in navigating the changing nature of work and achieving contentment in their careers.

13.5 SHIFTING SOCIETAL VALUES AND THE REDEFINITION OF SUCCESS

Societal values are constantly evolving, and the definitions of success, contentment, and growth are likely to change in response to new cultural, economic, and environmental realities. Understanding these shifts can help us envision a future where contentment and growth are redefined in more meaningful and sustainable ways.

The Rise of Well-Being and Purpose as Indicators of Success

Traditional indicators of success, such as wealth, status, and power, may give way to new measures that prioritize well-being, purpose, and community. As people become more aware of the limitations of material growth, they may seek fulfillment in non-material pursuits.

Potential Scenarios

- **Redefining Success Beyond Economic Measures**: Societies may adopt new indicators of success, such as Gross National Happiness, well-being indexes, or environmental health metrics.
- **Greater Focus on Purpose and Contribution**: Individuals may prioritize careers and activities that contribute to social good, environmental sustainability, and personal meaning.
- **A Shift Toward Minimalism and Simplicity**: There may be a growing movement toward minimalism, simplicity, and voluntary simplicity, where people seek contentment through experiences, relationships, and inner growth rather than material accumulation.

These shifts in values could lead to a more balanced approach to contentment and growth, where personal satisfaction is aligned with collective well-being and sustainability.

13.6 POTENTIAL PARADIGM SHIFTS: REIMAGINING CONTENTMENT AND GROWTH IN THE FUTURE

The future of contentment and growth may involve paradigm shifts that redefine how we pursue fulfillment and progress. These shifts could include:

1. **From Individualism to Interdependence**: A growing recognition of interdependence and interconnectedness could lead to a focus on collective well-being and shared growth, rather than individual achievement.
2. **From Economic Growth to Ecological Balance**: Economic growth may be redefined in terms of ecological balance and sustainability, with a focus on maintaining planetary health and supporting regenerative practices.
3. **From External Success to Inner Fulfillment**: Success and growth could be reimagined as inner fulfillment, personal development, and spiritual growth, shifting the emphasis from external achievements to inner well-being.

4. **From Technological Optimism to Mindful Integration**: Technology's role in contentment and growth may shift from unbridled optimism to mindful integration, where technological advancements are used to enhance human well-being while mitigating negative impacts.

These potential shifts offer a vision of a future where contentment and growth are not in opposition but are harmonized in ways that support both individual and collective thriving.

Conclusion: Reflecting on the Complexities of Contentment and Growth

Throughout this book, we have explored the multifaceted relationship between contentment and growth, delving into its philosophical, psychological, societal, economic, biological, and ethical dimensions. The journey has taken us through ancient wisdom, modern theories, personal stories, and futuristic scenarios, all with the aim of understanding how these seemingly opposing forces interact to shape our lives and society.

The question of whether contentment is the death of growth—or whether growth is incomplete without contentment—remains as complex and nuanced as ever. What we have seen is that there is no one-size-fits-all answer. Contentment and growth are not mutually exclusive; rather, they exist in a delicate balance, where each informs and influences the other.

Key Reflections

1. **The Paradox of Contentment and Growth**: As individuals, we are constantly navigating the paradox of wanting more while being satisfied with what we have. This tension drives us to seek out new experiences and accomplishments, yet it also teaches us the value of pausing, reflecting, and appreciating the present.
2. **Societal and Cultural Influences**: Our understanding of contentment and growth is shaped by the societal and cultural contexts in which we live. What is considered growth in one society may be viewed as overindulgence in another. Similarly, contentment may be seen as a virtue or a sign of complacency, depending on the cultural lens.

3. **Ethics and Responsibility**: The pursuit of growth, whether personal or societal, comes with ethical considerations. Growth that disregards the well-being of others or the environment is not true progress. Likewise, contentment that is achieved by turning a blind eye to injustice is not genuine peace.
4. **The Role of Technology and Innovation**: Technology has the power to transform our understanding of contentment and growth, offering new tools for personal development and societal progress. Yet, it also presents new challenges, such as maintaining human connection in a digital world or managing the impact of automation on employment.
5. **Future Directions**: As we look to the future, the definitions of contentment and growth are likely to evolve. Emerging trends, such as sustainable development, mindfulness movements, and reimagined work structures, suggest that we are entering a new era where the balance between these forces will be continually redefined.

FINAL THOUGHTS

Ultimately, contentment and growth are not destinations but ongoing processes. They are intertwined in a dance that reflects the complexities of human nature and the world we inhabit. Achieving harmony between these forces requires self-awareness, intentional choices, and a willingness to embrace both the aspirations that drive us and the moments of peace that ground us.

As you reflect on the themes and ideas presented in this book, I encourage you to consider your own relationship with contentment and growth. How do you define these concepts in your life? What drives you to strive for more, and what brings you a sense of fulfillment? There are no right or wrong answers—only the insights that emerge from your own experiences and reflections.

May this book inspire you to explore these questions with curiosity and openness, and may it serve as a guide on your journey toward a balanced and meaningful life. The pursuit of contentment and growth is yours to define, and the path you choose is uniquely your own.

REFERENCES

1. **Dweck, C. S. (2006).** *Mindset: The New Psychology of Success.* New York, NY: Random House.
    - This book explores the concept of fixed and growth mindsets and how adopting a growth mindset can lead to success and personal development.
2. **Csikszentmihalyi, M. (1990).** *Flow: The Psychology of Optimal Experience.* New York, NY: Harper & Row.
    - Introduces the concept of flow, a state of deep concentration and engagement, and its role in creativity and fulfillment.
3. **Schwartz, B. (2004).** *The Paradox of Choice: Why More is Less.* New York, NY: Ecco.
    - Discusses how having too many choices can lead to anxiety and dissatisfaction, affecting our ability to experience contentment.
4. **Neff, K. D. (2011).** *Self-Compassion: The Proven Power of Being Kind to Yourself.* New York, NY: William Morrow Paperbacks.
    - Explores the importance of self-compassion in achieving emotional resilience and well-being.
5. **Easterlin, R. A. (1974).** *Does Economic Growth Improve the Human Lot? Some Empirical Evidence.* In *Nations and Households in Economic Growth: Essays in Honor of Moses Abramovitz* (pp. 89–125). Academic Press.
    - Introduces the Easterlin Paradox, which examines the relationship between income and happiness.

6. **World Commission on Environment and Development (1987).** *Our Common Future.* Oxford: Oxford University Press.
   - Popularizes the concept of sustainable development, defined as meeting the needs of the present without compromising the ability of future generations to meet their own needs.
7. **Hardin, G. (1968).** *The Tragedy of the Commons. Science,* 162(3859), 1243–1248.
   - Describes the dilemma of shared resources being depleted by individual self-interest, highlighting the need for collective responsibility.
8. **Seligman, M. E. P. (2011).** *Flourish: A Visionary New Understanding of Happiness and Well-being.* New York, NY: Atria Books.
   - Explores the elements of well-being and introduces the PERMA model: Positive Emotions, Engagement, Relationships, Meaning, and Accomplishment.
9. **Sen, A. (1999).** *Development as Freedom.* Oxford: Oxford University Press.
   - Discusses development in terms of expanding human capabilities and freedoms rather than merely increasing economic growth.
10. **Kahneman, D., & Deaton, A. (2010).** *High Income Improves Evaluation of Life But Not Emotional Well-being. Proceedings of the National Academy of Sciences,* 107(38), 16489–16493.
    - Examines the impact of income on different aspects of well-being, highlighting that higher income improves life evaluation but not day-to-day emotional well-being.
11. **Goleman, D. (1995).** *Emotional Intelligence: Why It Can Matter More Than IQ.* New York, NY: Bantam Books.
    - Explores the role of emotional intelligence in personal and professional success and how it influences contentment and relationships.

12. **Bhutan Gross National Happiness Commission (2012).** *Gross National Happiness Index: 2012 Report.* Thimphu, Bhutan.
    - Provides insights into Bhutan's unique approach to measuring national progress through the Gross National Happiness Index, which considers environmental, social, and cultural factors.
13. **Clear, J. (2018).** *Atomic Habits: An Easy & Proven Way to Build Good Habits & Break Bad Ones.* New York, NY: Avery.
    - Offers strategies for forming positive habits and breaking negative ones, emphasizing the power of small, consistent changes.
14. **Rifkin, J. (2011).** *The Third Industrial Revolution: How Lateral Power is Transforming Energy, the Economy, and the World.* New York, NY: Palgrave Macmillan.
    - Discusses the role of technology and renewable energy in reshaping economic growth and societal development.
15. **Bhagavad Gita (Translated by Eknath Easwaran, 2007).** Tomales, CA: Nilgiri Press.
    - Provides spiritual guidance on achieving balance, contentment, and personal growth through detachment and selfless action.

AUTHOR: TANMEEN MAKEN

Tanmeen Maken, born in Pathankot, India, is a successful entrepreneur and an insightful thinker with a deep curiosity for understanding human nature. With a background in cement manufacturing and hydroelectric power projects, Tanmeen's professional success is complemented by his keen interest in exploring the complexities of human behavior and the paradoxes that shape our lives.

Driven by a relentless desire to delve deeper into the motives behind people's actions and choices, Tanmeen's writing is a reflection of his analytical mindset and his ability to question conventional beliefs. His unique perspective allows him to navigate themes like ambition, satisfaction, and personal growth, presenting them in a way that resonates with readers seeking clarity and balance in their own lives.

This debut book is a testament to his passion for unraveling the intricate dynamics of contentment and growth. Tanmeen invites readers to join him on a journey of self-discovery and introspection. His thoughtful observations and relatable narratives inspire readers to look beyond societal norms and embrace the contradictions that define the human experience.

www.ingramcontent.com/pod-product-compliance
Lightning Source LLC
LaVergne TN
LVHW091108150826
845673LV00002B/752

* 9 7 9 8 8 9 5 8 8 3 9 7 6 *